THE KING AND MRS. SIMPSON

The True Story of the Commoner Who Captured the Heart of a King

ERIN SCHULZ

WS BEETLE
&COMPANY

Library of Congress Cataloging-in-Publication Data
Names: Schulz, Erin Frances, (1975-) author
Title: The King & Mrs. Simpson, Second edition.

Identifiers:
LCCN 2018905327
ISBN 9790979178306 (1st edition, 2008, Paperback)
ISBN 9780979178351 (2nd edition, 2018, Hardcover)
ISBN 9780979178399 (2nd edition, 2018, Paperback)
ISBN 9780979178320 (2nd edition, 2018, ebook)

Cover design © Janet Schulz
Photograph Credit: Cecil Beaton (1904-1980)
The Duke & Duchess of Windsor
Silver Gelatin Print - England, 1938 V&A Images/Victoria & Albert
Museum, London, England

For my mom
with eternal love & gratitude

CONTENTS

AUTHOR'S NOTE

This small book is not a definitive biography of either the Duke or Duchess of Windsor, nor is it an analysis of the mid-twentieth century abdication crisis in Great Britain. Instead, it is the story of a love affair that for a shocking moment in 1936 captured the attention of the world. All the dialogue included in this book are the words of the Duke and Duchess of Windsor as quoted in their memoirs and in published letters released after the duchess's death in 1986. The use of the Duke and Duchess of Windsor's memoirs and letters as primary sources was intentional. *The King and Mrs. Simpson*, though researched extensively, is the story as the Duke and Duchess of Windsor wanted it to be told. The objective is to present a work of creative nonfiction that eliminates the extraneous material often found in traditional biographies. *The King and Mrs. Simpson* provides a snapshot of a poignant moment in the past, and hopefully an introduction to a romance that continues to fascinate readers today.

PROLOGUE

On December 10, 1936, King Edward VIII of Great Britain renounced his throne and his kingdom because he wanted to marry a woman considered unfit to be queen. She was an upper-middle class American divorcee named Wallis Warfield Spencer Simpson. The king's abdication, for which apparently the sole reason was love, shocked the world and ultimately sent him into exile for the rest of his life. For his subjects, hovering as they were on the eve of another unimaginable war, the name Mrs. Simpson stood for everything that was lost with the downfall of their beloved and charismatic king.

The ex-king married Wallis Simpson on June 3, 1937, and they were thereafter titled the Duke and Duchess of Windsor. The Duke of Windsor's brother, the quiet and conservative Prince Albert, father of Queen Elizabeth II, inherited the throne in his place and became known as King George VI.

Even nearly a century later, terrible anecdotes are still written about Mrs. Simpson. Had she been classically beautiful, her pedigree aristocratic, her glamour less exotic, her vivaciousness less threatening, it is possible the king's passion for her would have been understood. Instead, their love affair has been chronicled as one of peculiarity. Mystery has surrounded their romance, and the worst of their detractors have hinted at the presence of raw political ambition, androgyne, and Nazi sympathies. The Duchess of Windsor is most often associated with vulgar wealth, drowned by an existence that revolved around fashion, jewelry, and parties. In modern films, she is portrayed on a spectrum from glamorous and outspoken (*W.E.*) to imperious and overbearing (*The King's Speech*).

Yet, the Duchess of Windsor had a deeper character than what appeared. She possessed remarkable gifts of survival and reinvention, and an ability to keep moving forward despite enormous odds. From the start, she faced hardship. Her father died when she was six months old, and she was raised in an environment of relative poverty, relying on charity from her wealthy family. As a young lady, she married a U.S. Navy officer expecting an adventurous life of travel, but she was devastated almost immediately by marital problems stemming from her husband's mental cruelty and physical abuse. After their divorce, which horrified her family, she tried looking for a job to support herself in an era when most women did not work, only to find the job market limited for someone with no practical skills. She then settled for a stable and possibly passionless marriage to her second husband, Ernest Simpson, and moved with him to London. Shortly after her second marriage, her mother died of a stroke leaving Wallis, who had no siblings, rather alone in the world, with the exception of her aunt, Bessie Merryman.

Homesick and sad in London, she tried to bolster her spirits and surroundings by refining her expertise in homemaking and entertaining. It was her unrelenting quest for a vibrant social life to fill her days and ease her loneliness that led her to cross paths with Edward, Prince of Wales, the heir to the British throne. A friendship began, and Wallis soon became his closest companion and greatest confidant.

The romance could have continued indefinitely in a private manner even after he became king had he not decided marrying her was essential to his very existence. His gallant insistence that she be his wife instead of his mistress ended up causing a crisis of the utmost magnitude for the monarchy.

They were married almost six months to the day of his abdication, on June 3, 1937. After their wedding, they were inseparable and remained so until the duke's death thirty-five years later. Since his abdication banished him from his home and his family, the duchess tried to recreate, through regal decoration and luxurious living, a life for the duke reminiscent of the glorious one he had led as prince and king. From all reports, he remained deeply in love with her until the end, never blaming her for his fateful decision or all that he had lost by choosing her over the throne. Whatever was the camaraderie that existed between them, it endured for more than forty years. Perhaps only time will eliminate the lingering mystery surrounding their relationship.

Perhaps it was just a love story after all.

❧ I ❧
DEPARTURE

December 3, 1936

On the edge of Windsor Great Park in England, a castle from a fairy tale is hidden by trees that keep its secrets mythic and clandestine. It is a childlike palace, a Gothic dwelling reminiscent of ancient wars, a fortress with beveled turrets, and a high tower that once flew the flag of a king.

The king was Edward VIII of Great Britain, Ireland, and the British Dominions beyond the Seas, Emperor of India, the former Prince of Wales, and at the time, the most exciting monarch ever to reign over the grandest empire in the world. His family and friends called him David. His castle was known as Fort Belvedere, but for him it was always just "the Fort."

On the evening of December 3, 1936, a light rain was falling as a car carrying Lord Brownlow, friend and equerry to King Edward, turned from the main road onto the Fort's unlit gravel drive, its headlights piercing the heavy winter mist and fog. The chauffeur parked the car on the circular drive in front of the fountain by the main door. The Fort was illuminated, but the warmth of the lights in the windows belied the heartbreak that was taking place inside. Recent events had caused turmoil for the monarchy, and the future of the king was in peril, not because of the usual demons of war or tyranny, but because of a woman.

Inside the Fort, a flurry of activity was taking place in the octagon-shaped drawing room, a room where great weekend parties used to be held, where guests once danced to music from a gramophone on the black and white marble floor. Now a melancholy sense of doom lingered in the air. All those present could not help but wonder if an enchanted time was slipping away.

The king had spent the day working on a speech he wanted to broadcast over the radio to the people of his empire. He knew radio was a powerful medium and one of the forces behind President Franklin D. Roosevelt's surging popularity in the United States. The king was convinced that if his subjects could only hear his side of the story in his own voice, then they would understand his unyielding desire to marry the woman he realized years before he could not live without.

The king – born at the end of the 19th century, who

had traveled the world, who had seen first-hand the horrors of war, who had witnessed the end of the Victorian era and the Edwardian era – considered himself a monarch of modernity, and one who should be able to marry for love rather than royal convenience. He was of course aware that his avant-garde ways sometimes caused controversy, but he also knew they were one of the reasons for his immense popularity. As long as he could remember, his subjects and the general public had adored him. Throngs of people across the world flocked to catch a glimpse of him every time he appeared in public, and women everywhere swooned over his good looks. He had blond hair, blue eyes, and a face that could rival any film star, although on this night, anguish and exhaustion had taken their toll. In the drawing room, he was chain-smoking and unable to sit still.

Also in the room, seated on the Chippendale furniture, was a striking American woman named Wallis Simpson. Her hair was short and glossy black, and she wore it in the latest style, parted in the middle with pin curls around her face. Her dark eyebrows framed large blue eyes set on a fine-boned, angular face. She had never been called beautiful, but her reed-thin figure and exquisite manner of dress projected a skeletal elegance. Amongst her friends, she was known for her vivaciousness and her spirited manner, but on this night her usual joie de vivre was gone. Even the presence of her Aunt

Bessie, who had traveled from the States to support her, was unable to provide her with consolation.

Her world was collapsing around her, and she was utterly powerless to stop the forces beyond her control. The British press, who had long honored a gentlemen's agreement with the king promising they would not report on his private affairs, had launched the story of their relationship. Her impending divorce became world news, and threats in the form of angry letters were flooding her mailbox, while protests took place in the streets. Fearing for her safety, she and the king decided it was best if she left the United Kingdom temporarily. Her housekeeper had returned to London earlier in the day to pack her clothes and the precious collection of jewelry the king had given to her over the years. In a state of panic, while the king worked on his radio speech, she drafted a will on the Fort's stationery.

Lord Brownlow's arrival prompted the servants to bring in a light dinner on trays, though no one at the Fort had an appetite, least of all Wallis or the king. Her planned departure time was fast approaching, and her escape was so fraught with danger it was forefront on everyone's mind.

Wallis, accompanied by Lord Brownlow, his chauffeur, and an Inspector from Scotland Yard were to be driven from the Fort to the port of Newhaven on the English Channel coast where they were booked on the ten o'clock evening ferry bound for Dieppe, France.

Once in France, they would drive south to Cannes where Wallis's longtime friends, Herman and Katherine Rogers, had a villa. In an attempt to confuse the press corps who were camped outside the Fort, a chauffeur named Ladbrook had already left in Wallis's Buick and headed toward London. Once he was sure he was no longer being followed, he was to turn the car around and head for the ferry to meet the rest of the party.

As the minutes ticked by, the mood remained solemn in the drawing room, and most of the food the servants brought in was left untouched. The king finally rose and thanked Lord Brownlow for his service and his promise to look after Wallis on the long journey south. Lord Brownlow tried to appear calm, but he was secretly brimming with trepidation. Unbeknownst to everyone at the Fort, he and several of the king's friends, had concocted an alternative plan for Wallis, and it was one they were convinced could save the monarchy. Fearing the king's objection, Lord Brownlow was waiting until he was alone with Wallis to explain their idea.

When the time finally came to leave, the king, depressed and anxious, led Wallis to the front door. Outside in the driveway, his servants were loading the last of her luggage into the waiting car. Lord Brownlow and Inspector Evans discreetly stepped aside and busied themselves with their own preparations to give the king and Wallis privacy.

After bidding farewell to Aunt Bessie, Wallis and the king embraced and stood for a moment holding each other closely in the glow of the foyer lights. Reluctantly Wallis slid into the backseat of the car, and the king reached in and touched her hand. "Wherever you reach tonight, no matter what time, telephone me," he said with tears in his eyes. "Bless you, my darling."

Inspector Evans put the Rolls Royce in gear, and the king watched as it moved slowly around the circular drive toward Windsor Great Park and was soon engulfed by the mist hanging low over the road. It was difficult for him not to recall all the summers he had spent in that very park, riding horses with his brothers, boating on the Upper Thames, and golfing on the grounds of Windsor Castle with his father. Now his life and his future, once promising and legendary, were in danger of descending into the wasteland of an abyss.

Aunt Bessie stood beside him silently until the car was gone. She had cared for Wallis like a second mother since Wallis was a child, and she had become even closer to Wallis after Wallis's mother died. She had also long questioned the king's intentions with her niece. From the onset, she often expressed to Wallis her fear that he would gravely hurt her. After all, standing beside her was a man who could have any woman of his choice. Wallis was from the wrong country and the wrong social class and she was already once divorced. Perhaps most upsetting for Aunt Bessie was that after years of witnessing her niece's heartache, Wallis had finally married a good man, Ernest Simpson, who cared deeply for her. Aunt Bessie didn't doubt that the king loved Wallis, but she was astonished by his actions. As each day passed, it was becoming increasingly apparent he would have to give up his throne in order to marry Wallis. For Aunt Bessie, the thought of the king tossing aside his throne was incomprehensible.

As if reading her mind, the king turned to face her. "I feel terribly sorry about all this. I hope you understand."

"In spite of everything, Sir, you are really determined to marry my niece?"

"I am."

"Even if it means giving up the Throne?"

"Yes, even if I have to abdicate. I hope that we shall be able to marry and that I can carry on my work as king. But I am determined in any case to marry her."

"Wallis can make you happy," she said, "if happiness is really what you want."

"It is a great deal, Mrs. Merryman."

"But isn't there perhaps something more? Your country? Are you right in putting your happiness before what your people may regard as your duty?"

"It is not a question merely of happiness. I cannot with a full heart carry out my duties in the loneliness that surrounds me."

He assured her he had already considered the consequences. He refused to relegate Wallis to the status of a mistress. He wanted Wallis to be his wife, to be bestowed with proper royal titles, and to live alongside him as queen. Besides, he had already proposed to her. He had encouraged her, persuaded her even, to file for divorce from Ernest.

Aunt Bessie had spoken to him many times before about Wallis. As they stood outside the Fort, she reminded him again that Wallis was a wonderful person, but also a woman who had struggled and persevered, who had remained warm and kind with a unique ability to see the bright side of things. A woman who had never lost her love of life. She wanted the king to take care of her as he had always promised he would.

What a pity, the king thought, *that those standing in judgment upon us could not have heard what Mrs. Merryman told me about Wallis, the American stranger against whom that night nearly every hand in Britain seemed turned.*

2

THE PRINCE

He saw her for the first time nearly six years before in Melton Mowbray at the country house of his girlfriend at the time, Lady Thelma Furness. He was the Prince of Wales then, and he later recalled the night was a typical winter evening in England—achingly cold, damp, and foggy. The prince and his younger brother, Prince George, arrived at the house at seven o'clock and as usual found a bevy of guests waiting to greet them. When they entered the brightly lit drawing room, tea was set up in front of the fireplace where everyone had gathered to stay warm.

There were almost thirty people in attendance that weekend, several friends from the hunting crowd and Thelma's brother-in-law, Benjamin Thaw. Benjamin had brought a young couple with him from London, Ernest

Simpson, a shipping executive, and Ernest's new wife, an American from Baltimore, Maryland, named Wallis.

Thelma made the rounds of introductions with the princes and eventually they came to the Simpsons. Ernest, a British-American who had long since sworn allegiance to the Crown, was thrilled by the chance to meet his future king. But the woman who stood beside her husband was less engaging. She was tiny in stature and sick with a terrible cold. She managed to curtsy gracefully despite having only learned to do so earlier that day on the train from London. Thelma casually introduced her as "Mrs. Simpson." In doing so, she quite unknowingly altered the course of the British monarchy forever.

It may not have been love at first sight, but something about Mrs. Simpson intrigued the Prince of Wales. He would later say, "From the first I looked upon her as the most independent women I had ever met."

Wallis Simpson, however, never expected to make any impression on him at all. She saw herself as what she was—a divorcée from the States, nearing middle age, who was newly remarried and trying to rebuild her life as the wife of an upper-middle class businessman. In contrast, the future king was a global celebrity, the great-grandson of Queen Victoria, the grandson of King Edward VII, the son of King George V and Queen Mary, and next in line to inherit the throne.

꧁꧂

PRINCE EDWARD ALBERT CHRISTIAN GEORGE ANDREW PATRICK DAVID was born on June 23, 1894, the eldest of six children, and destined by order of birth for greatness of an extraordinary magnitude. His birth was celebrated around the world and his childhood was one of confined splendor. His parents moved with the seasons between grand family houses on the estates of Sandringham and Windsor, Frogmore and Balmoral.

Growing up, the young prince who was called by his seventh name, David, loved the outdoors, admired and feared his father, and disliked formal education. Because of his position, he socialized only with his immediate family. His parents were aloof by nature. They accepted their majestic duty to the United Kingdom of Great Britain without question or hesitation. Prince Edward was always reminded of his birthright, and he was made to understand that his mission in life was to be of service to a kingdom and an empire that spanned the far reaches of the globe.

The prince first ventured beyond his protective cocoon at age thirteen when he was sent to become a cadet at the Royal Naval College on the Isle of Wight. Although he was called Cadet Prince Edward, everyone there was instructed not to treat him with special privilege, as King George did not want him to behave with entitlement.

Initially, the other boys hazed him. They pulled such pranks as pouring red ink into his hair and closing a window on his head to mimic a guillotine. But the prince, much to everyone's surprise, was lighthearted. Rather than crying, he laughed and played along with their games. Before long he had made the first true friends outside his family he had ever known.

Still, his different station in life could not be ignored. His school, the Royal Naval College, was on the grounds of Queen Victoria's summer mansion, Osborne, which loomed in the distance. On holidays, he returned to a palace, while his classmates returned to modest homes. The other boys there were being groomed for military careers aboard ships. His career was to be aboard a throne. And when his uncle, Czar Nicholas II of Russia, arrived on the Isle of Wight on the royal Russian yacht *Standart* flanked by nearly one hundred warships, it was Prince Edward who was invited to host them as they stopped briefly to tour the magnificent halls of Osborne.

When he was fifteen, his grandfather, King Edward VII died, and his father inherited the throne. He was titled King George V, and his mother was titled Queen Mary. Prince Edward became the Heir Apparent. Nothing now, or so he thought, would prevent him from one day becoming "by the Grace of God, of Great Britain, Ireland, and the British Dominions beyond the Seas, King, Defender of the Faith, Emperor of India."

The following year, on his sixteenth birthday, King George bestowed on Prince Edward the title Prince of Wales. He also gave him three tasks to accomplish. The prince had to spend extensive time in France and Germany to perfect the languages of those countries, and to be introduced to the history and culture of Great Britain's two closest rivals. He had to attend the University of Oxford to complete his formal education, and he had to give up the Royal Navy for good. His father's commands, though not entirely unexpected, were still distressing for him. He had always known one day he would have to resign from the Royal Navy. Oxford, however, was a dreaded surprise. The thought of formal education was horrifying to him after the excitement and adventure of military training.

As the prince expected, his years at Oxford were painful. It started with the British press who made a spectacle of his arrival. He was embarrassed that he had been required to bring a butler and tutor, and further mortified to discover his dormitory room had been redesigned in a manner believed to befit a prince. Even worse was the fact that his naval training had left him behind his new classmates in traditional studies. Bored and ill prepared for the rigorous academic courses, he spent much of his time drinking and improving his horseback riding skills.

In June of 1914, everything seemed peaceful and calm as the summer began. The prince was nearing age twenty, and his father finally agreed to let him withdraw from Oxford to continue his education in the Army's Officer Training Corps. The prince hoped to be able to join a military unit called the Grenadier Guards the following January. But five days after his birthday, Archduke Franz Ferdinand, heir to the throne of the Austro-Hungarian empire, and his wife, Countess Sophie, were assassinated as they toured Sarajevo in open car. The double murder set off a chain of events that ultimately culminated in the start of World War I.

☙❧

ON THAT FATEFUL DAY IN JUNE, THE ARCHDUKE AND Countess had attended Mass earlier that morning in Sarajevo before leaving for a reception downtown. The Archduke knew the risk he was taking traveling in a convertible, but he insisted on minimum security to add an aura of confidence to his trip. As their motorcade traveled through the crowded downtown streets, five assassins disguised as onlookers waited patiently for their moment to strike.

The first assassin tossed a bomb at the Archduke's car as it passed through an area called the Appel Embankment, but the bomb bounced off the hood and detonated on the ground bringing the motorcade to an abrupt halt. Police chased the bomber who tried to escape by jumping into the river. Meanwhile, three of the other assassins panicked and fled the scene. The fifth and last remaining assassin, a Bosnian-Serb named Gavrilo Princip, who had orchestrated the entire affair, witnessed the botched scene unfold. Instead of trying to hide, he remained frozen on the Appel Embankment.

The Archduke and Countess, shaken yet unharmed, continued to the town hall for the reception. After the reception, things were progressing smoothly until their driver made a wrong turn and had to stop the car in order to turn around. The entire moment might have been lost to time had the wrong turn not occurred directly in front of Gavrilo Princip. He fired his pistol twice, hitting the Archduke first and the Countess second. Both died within the half hour.

In retaliation for the murder of their royal family, Austria-Hungary turned to their ally, Germany, for support before declaring war on Serbia. And since Serbia was aligned with Russia, Czar Nicholas II had little choice but to mobilize troops to defend Serbia. Compounding matters was France's alliance with Russia, so they too mobilized against Austria-Hungary and Germany.

Diplomats tried in vain to defuse the situation, yet by the end of July, Kaiser Wilhelm II of Germany, under pressure from his generals, ordered his troops to march on Serbia and organize a battle plan to invade France.

In Great Britain, troops were called to arms to

rescue France. The prince desperately wanted to partici-
pate in the coming action, but he was sequestered in
London by monarchical authorities who feared he
would be kidnapped or killed, leaving him unbearably
frustrated. He had grown up hearing stories of Queen
Victoria's wars in India and Africa, and he was enough
of an empire builder at heart to want to fight for his
homeland. His contemporaries and many of his Navy
friends were already heading to the front lines in
France.

The ensuing conflict would, erroneously as it turned
out, be called the "War to End All Wars." Astonishingly,
three of the major powers involved, King George V of
England, Kaiser Wilhelm II of Germany, and Czar
Nicholas II of Russia, were cousins who could trace
their ancestry directly to Queen Victoria. They had
maintained regular and friendly correspondence prior to
1914, despite the competitive mindset that permeated
the monarchs in Europe and the United Kingdom.

The German army moved with amazing speed
throughout the Continent considering most of their
equipment was pulled by horses. They outflanked
French fortifications by marching through neutral
Belgium before turning south to head for Paris. When
they were almost within sight of the city, the Germans
hesitated, giving the French army time to regroup and
position themselves between the Germans and Paris.
Both sides started to build a series of hand-dug trenches

to ward off attacks. The trenches eventually stretched from east to west across the entire country. The conditions in the trenches were deplorable, and the combination of rain, mud, and unsanitary conditions caused thousands to die from dysentery and exposure. For four long years, the soldiers hovered on what was termed the "Western Front."

The situation was no better in the east where the Germans, Russians, Austrians, Italians, Turks, and Serbians were fighting each other over thousands of miles of rough terrain and mountains. Nationalism for homelands swept across the civilized globe. Every country, even those under empire domination, clung to their flags as though they were sacred objects. Parades became national pastimes, and military bands raised the spirits of the local population.

As the war progressed, the prince never stopped begging his father to allow him to join the effort. As soon as his father relented, the prince left London and headed straight for France. He was sorely disappointed when he arrived and found the fear for his safety left him assigned to desk jobs consisting of routine paperwork and menial tasks.

Humiliated by his special treatment, and ashamed every time he received a medal he felt he didn't deserve, the prince took matters into his own hands. He began to ride a bicycle through the army camps and into the trenches where his presence instantly boosted the morale of many British soldiers. His effort to play an active role in the British campaign, and his desire to live alongside his comrades in the trenches, endeared him to his subjects even more so than before.

IN 1915, THE GERMANS, WHO WERE CONVINCED THEIR enemies were shipping munitions on passenger ocean liners, torpedoed and sunk the British yacht *Lusitania* off the coast of Ireland, killing over one thousand civilians.

The tragedy caused anti-war sentiments to wane. In the United States, a great deal of propaganda about alleged German atrocities was spread to sway public opinion in favor of the war. By April of 1917, President Woodrow Wilson was finally pressured to declare war on Germany. The tiny, ill-equipped United States army presented little military threat to their enemies, but the psychological impact of the United States joining the war proved to be significant.

A year and a half later, with the German army weakened, and all sides exhausted and saddened by the ongoing battles and loss of life, diplomats once again tried to bring the war to a close. On November 18, 1918, an armistice was signed to end the war. Fighting continued in small pockets in the east, but the war was essentially over. The Germans believed they had signed a peace treaty, but by the time the Paris Peace Conference was held in 1919, they realized they had actually signed a document of surrender. Kaiser Wilhelm was forced to abdicate, and he spent the rest of his life exiled in the Netherlands.

The Russian monarchy had already ended with the assassination of Czar Nicholas II and his family in 1918. The Austro-Hungarian Empire was disbanded, and new republics were formed in its place. The staggering human loss from 1914 to 1918 was unparalleled in the history of warfare. Over fifteen million people were killed, wounded, or died of disease.

The British monarchy survived intact, but a dark cloud hung over the island nation because an entire generation of young men had been killed in battle. One bright light remained. In February of 1919, the Prince of Wales, now more popular than ever before, returned home from the war ready to begin life anew. When he turned twenty-five that June, he knew the time had come for him to start working on his princely duties. He was bothered because he couldn't help but feel they were rather shallow after the impact of the war. He wanted to do something unique, something more than just attend honorary ceremonies and perform charity work.

He consulted with his father and the prime minister, David Lloyd George, and they decided he should travel the world as a "Goodwill Ambassador." The British

Empire may have survived the war, but its power and influence had suffered. The king and prime minister were convinced the presence of the young, charismatic prince would help their colonies maintain loyalty to Great Britain.

The prince left Portsmouth, England in August of 1919, on a battleship outfitted for him and his travel staff. They sailed across the Atlantic to Newfoundland, giving him his first look at the continent he still called the "New World." He sailed on to Quebec City, then traveled by train to Washington, D.C. where he paid a visit to the dying President Wilson. From D.C., he headed north by train to New Jersey, and crossed the Hudson River on an admiral's ship. Waiting yachts in New York City's harbor blew their whistles to welcome him. As he made his way up Broadway in Manhattan, onlookers in the windows of the office towers above him tossed ticker tape at his motorcade in celebration. He toured City Hall, Grant's Tomb, the Stock Exchange, and attended the opera and the Ziegfeld Follies. He later said the visit instilled in him a love for America that would endure throughout his lifetime.

When the prince finally returned home, his tour was heralded as a great success. It had special meaning for him as well. His long days at sea had given him time to reflect on his own place in the future of the monarchy, and the dire need for modernization in the British

Empire. He decided that when his time came to rule, he would be a different sort of king.

In the meantime, he found himself suddenly cast into the role of the most eligible bachelor in the world. King George and Queen Mary were pressuring him to settle down, and they expressed concern over his playboy lifestyle and his evident love of the nightlife. They hoped he would soon marry one of the eligible ladies of the aristocracy, but the prince insisted he would only marry for love. He was looking for more than just a companion of convenience, and he longed to find someone who would understand him and share his duties. He also wanted a woman whose temperament was kindhearted and warm, as opposed to his mother who tended to be distant and austere. He had developed a penchant for older women who he found more interesting than coming-of-age European princesses. He felt they possessed the skills he highly admired, such as entertaining and keeping a beautiful, organized house.

His great love of the 1920s was a beautiful commoner named Freda Dudley Ward. She was married to a member of Parliament and had two young children. Freda listened to him, offered advice, and helped him with the restoration of Fort Belvedere that his father had recently gifted to him to use as a country retreat.

When his relationship with Freda tapered off into friendship, the prince fell in love with another married woman, Lady Thelma Furness, a socialite and former actress. On the second weekend of January 1931, Thelma hosted a party at her country house north of London. Thelma's sister, Connie, was unable to attend but Connie's husband, Benjamin, planned to go. Not wanting Benjamin to make the lengthy train journey alone, Connie asked Thelma if a charming couple she knew from London could accompany Benjamin in her place. Connie was quite certain Thelma may have even met them before. Their names are the Simpsons, she told Thelma. Ernest and his new American wife, Wallis.

WALLIS

H er story begins in the summer of 1896 in the Blue Ridge Mountains of Pennsylvania. Bessie Wallis Warfield was born on June 19th to T. Wallis Warfield and his beautiful wife, Alice Montague Warfield, a young couple from Baltimore. They were vacationing there in the hopes that the crisp mountain air would lessen the pain of tuberculosis that was slowly killing T. Wallis. T. Wallis and Alice were deeply in love, but they had married against the wishes of their wealthy families. Bessie Wallis, or "Wallis" as she was called, would be their only child as just five months after she was born, T. Wallis succumbed to his disease.

When T. Wallis died, Alice was nearly destitute. Shunned by her own family who was still angry over her marriage, she was forced to move into the third floor of her mother-in-law's mansion in a prosperous section of Baltimore. The move would prove to be a positive experience for Wallis because her grandmother's influence made a lasting impression on her. Anna Warfield was a strict perfectionist who taught Wallis the proper etiquette, grooming, and deportment that would remain with her throughout her lifetime.

Also living in the house was T. Wallis's brother, Solomon. Solomon was a successful banker and prominent Baltimore citizen. Since he was a bachelor, he began to help support Alice and Wallis financially, though his generosity was sporadic and unreliable.

When Wallis was five years old, Alice suddenly informed her they were moving to a hotel nearby. Wallis was too young to understand that Solomon had fallen in love with her mother. The prospect of her older son marrying his dead brother's wife was too much for Anna Warfield to bear. For Alice, being asked to leave the mansion was not terrible news as she had greatly loved the gentle T. Wallis and could not envision a union with his controlling brother.

For seven years, Wallis and her mother were adrift in Baltimore, but they continued to visit Anna and Solomon, who maintained his financial assistance despite his failed romance with Alice. They lived in hotels and apartment houses, and also stayed with Alice's sister, Bessie Merryman. Alice found work as a dressmaker and a cook, and in her free time she sewed the latest fashions for Wallis so Wallis would be dressed as well as the other girls at the private schools Solomon funded.

In 1908, when Wallis was twelve years old, Alice remarried an affluent man named John Rasin, whose ample trust fund eliminated his need to hold a job. The new family moved into a three-story brownstone, and Alice, finally secure after more than a decade, began to entertain lavishly.

When Wallis turned sixteen, her stepfather agreed to pay the tuition for Oldfields, a finishing school for girls located twenty miles north of downtown Baltimore. Her lessons were structured around religion and the motto that "Gentleness and Courtesy Are Expected of the Girls at all Times." At Oldfields, Wallis was further introduced to the moneyed, aristocratic set, although unlike the other girls, she had no assurance of an inheritance of her own. Her future wealth was entirely dependent on the whims of her stepfather and Solomon.

In the spring of her first year at school, John Rasin passed away unexpectedly from Bright's disease. Wallis rushed home to Baltimore and found her mother inconsolable. The death of her second husband devastated her emotionally and physically. Adding to her pain was the fact that John had never changed his will to provide for his wife and stepdaughter after his death. Once again, they had to turn to Solomon for support.

Solomon allowed Wallis to return to Oldfields for her final year. She graduated in May of 1914, one month before her eighteenth birthday. Wallis had grown into a vivacious, charismatic, and striking young woman. She wore her hair short with loose curls, applied make-up to flatter her large blue eyes, and preferred clothes that showcased her very thin figure. She had also mastered flirtatious mannerisms that made her the life of every party. Instead of being demure and prim, she was outgoing, forthright, and popular, and the boys of Baltimore adored her.

After Oldfields, she was looking forward to becoming a debutante in Baltimore with the other girls of her social set. After witnessing her mother's plight for so long, Wallis yearned for her own security and independence from Solomon. Her goal was to find a wealthy husband so she could spend the rest of her days as a respectable society wife. Everything might have worked out as planned for her except there was a looming catastrophe in Europe. Shortly after her eighteenth birthday, Archduke Franz Ferdinand and Countess Sophie were just stepping into their open car for their tour of Sarajevo.

As the war was spreading throughout Europe, Wallis was spending her time going out on dates, attending tea parties, and designing the dress her mother would sew for her for the Bachelor's Cotillion, the grandest debutante ball of the season. For the society ladies of Baltimore, the war was happening somewhere very far away. Solomon, however, was disturbed by what he considered blatant disregard for the catastrophe in Europe. To show his support for the troops, he refused to throw a debutante ball party in Wallis's honor as was customary, even going as far as publishing a mention in the local newspaper stating that the ball would not take place. Wallis was deeply embarrassed, but she tried to enjoy what was supposed to be a special time in her life.

Then in December, her grandmother contracted pneumonia and died shortly thereafter, putting an abrupt end to Wallis's days as a debutante. The Warfield family went into mourning and ceased all of their social activities. Wallis was gravely hurt by the loss of her grandmother. Even though they had not been close for the last several years, Wallis had long admired her grandmother's sense of self and iron will.

After several months of mourning, Wallis was aching for a change from dreary Baltimore. Her cousin Corinne was married to a United States Naval Officer who was the commander of the new Pensacola Naval Air Station in Florida. Corinne invited Wallis to stay with her for an extended vacation, and Wallis thought the idea was wonderful. It would be warm in Florida, and there would be plenty of palm trees, beaches, and most importantly, available men. Wallis begged her mother and Solomon to allow her to go. In April of

1916, they finally relented, and Wallis boarded a train bound for Pensacola.

Wallis blossomed in Florida. The sun was shining every day, the evenings were pleasant and long, and the air was filled with a pervasive sense of adventure. Aviation was a new field in 1916, and aviators were considered daring and courageous. Corinne seemed to be leading a much more glamorous life than Wallis's friends back in Baltimore—a life filled with travel, excitement, and handsome officers.

On Wallis's second day in Pensacola, a few of the officers stopped by Corinne's house for lunch. One dark-haired officer in particular caught Wallis's attention. His name was Earl Winfield Spencer, Jr., though everyone called him Win. He was from Chicago and was a graduate of the Naval Academy in Annapolis. Wallis had never met anyone like him. She found him much more fascinating than the boys she knew at home, and she fell in love almost instantly. Win was taken with Wallis as well. The first day they talked nonstop throughout lunch and afterwards Win asked if he could see her again.

Win began to take Wallis dancing every night at the nearby San Juan Hotel, and he escorted her to parties and luncheons during the day when he wasn't working. He also brought her to the local country club to teach her how to play golf. Win was attracted to danger and Wallis listened for hours as he discussed every last detail of aviation, including, to her horror, graphic descriptions of crashes.

By 1916, everyone knew it was only a matter of time before the United States became involved in World War I. Win longed to be a part of the action, and he was certain he would soon be sent to Europe to fly. He also wanted to get married before he left.

One evening after a movie, as they were sitting on the porch of the country club enjoying the night air, Win asked Wallis to marry him. Wallis was ecstatic. She had suspected a proposal was coming, but she was slightly nervous because their romance had happened so quickly.

Corinne was thrilled by their engagement. Despite the war, she believed a naval officer was a perfect match for someone as dynamic as Wallis. Win could offer Wallis a chance to see the world beyond Baltimore. Although he wasn't wealthy, his Navy pay was substantial enough for them to be comfortable. Wallis would have an opportunity to enjoy the nomadic military life and the social responsibilities that came with being an officer's wife.

Wallis returned to Baltimore to tell her mother and Solomon she was engaged, and she wasn't surprised when they expressed their concerns. Win had a dangerous career that might put him on the front lines of the war. He was also not financially independent. Her mother and Solomon had hoped Wallis would marry a prominent businessman or an heir to a Baltimore fortune. But Wallis insisted the life of a Navy wife was the one she wanted. Alice and Solomon remained skeptical until Win, looking formal and distinguished in his uniform, arrived in Baltimore to meet them. The confidence he exuded managed to charm even Solomon.

Wallis and Win were married on November 8, 1916, a mere seven months after they met in Pensacola. Win stood at the altar in his full-dress uniform, and Wallis wore a white velvet dress embroidered with pearls. After the ceremony, the newlyweds proceeded out of the church under crossed swords held over their heads by Win's fellow officers.

Wallis was certain she was about to embark on the most exciting adventure of her life, but soon after their wedding things took a dark turn. Win suffered from a brooding, competitive temperament and a frightening tendency toward jealousy. He also suffered from a drinking problem. In Pensacola, Wallis had seen Win drink to excess with the other officers, but she'd dismissed it as a coping mechanism to relax after the danger and thrill of flying. But on their honeymoon, she started to realize Win's drinking was less of a social pastime and more of a precarious dependency.

When they returned to Pensacola, Wallis was determined to settle into her role as a Navy wife. She and Win enjoyed several months of relative tranquility until the United States finally declared war on Germany on

April 6, 1917. Win expected to be awarded an aerial combat job overseas, so he was shocked and dismayed when he was posted to Boston instead, assigned with the task of building a small naval air station. He was devastated and perplexed by the news, but Wallis suspected his drinking and behavioral problems had cost him the posting to Europe.

They moved to Massachusetts in May of 1917, and Win tried to keep his drinking under control and prove himself worthy of an assignment on the front lines in Europe. As Win constructed and organized the Squantum Naval Air Base, Wallis tried to enjoy her time in Boston even though she found it a difficult place to make friends. She spent the majority of her days touring the city, reading the newspaper front-to-back, and perfecting her role as a homemaker.

In October of 1917, Win received word he was being transferred again, this time to San Diego to construct and command the North Island Naval Air Station. Once again, he was outraged. He had assumed if he succeeded in Boston, he would be sent overseas to fly, but the Navy found his skills better suited to building and expanding domestic bases.

Wallis was secretly thrilled by his transfer. She set about packing up their apartment and organizing their move across the country. When she finally arrived in San Diego after a long rail journey, she immediately found California sunny and inviting. They had rented a bungalow, and Wallis relished the task of setting up her new home. She hoped California, with its climate reminiscent of their early days in Pensacola, would be a fresh start for her and Win.

Sadly, it was not to be. Win was frustrated and unhappy in his new position, which he considered a career setback. He started drinking heavily again and his combative temperament returned. He instigated fights with Wallis over trivial matters and even locked her in her room so he could go out without her. He also began staying out late at night, sometimes failing to return home at all. Distraught and ashamed, Wallis confided her marital troubles to no one. Instead, she took comfort in organizing her house and trying to learn how to cook. As the wife of the commanding officer, she was expected to put up a good front in public, so she tried to settle into a social routine with the other Navy wives.

THE WAR ENDED ON NOVEMBER 11, 1918. PEOPLE danced in the streets of San Diego and the celebration continued for days, but Win's dream of playing a significant role in the war was dashed forever. Hoping to lift his spirits Wallis suggested he consider a career in commercial aviation, which was a burgeoning field at the time, but Win had no interest in leaving the Navy.

Wallis was disappointed, because as exciting as the Navy had been at first, its appeal was diminishing for her. She yearned to settle down permanently somewhere and perhaps even salvage her marriage if Win found a new, fulfilling career. Since Win would not consider resigning from the Navy, they remained in San Diego, living in their small bungalow in Coronado.

In May of 1921, Win was posted to Washington, D.C. to help create the new Bureau of Aeronautics. Wallis was relieved he had been assigned to an important position, and she was happy she was going home to the East Coast. But Washington, D.C. was not a fresh start for them either. Win's drunken rages continued at night, only this time they were not in the privacy of their bungalow, but in a hotel with thin walls. Win was unwilling to seek help, and Wallis was too embarrassed to confide in anyone, not even her mother or Aunt Bessie, even though both ladies now lived nearby.

The breaking point came one Sunday afternoon. While Wallis was in the bathroom, Win locked the door from the outside and left the apartment. She was trapped for hours and too terrified to move or call out for help. For the first time, Wallis began to contemplate divorce, even though she knew it would bring dishonor to her family.

Shortly after the bathroom incident, Wallis packed her bags and moved into her mother's apartment. As she expected, her family expressed shock when she announced she was filing for divorce. They reminded her she was only twenty-four years old, and no one in her family had ever divorced. Her mother urged her to try again. Aunt Bessie lectured her on the stigma of being a divorcee with no immediate prospects for remarriage. Solomon strictly forbade her to go through with it and threatened to remove her from his will.

To Wallis's surprise, Win was remorseful. "Wallis, I've had it coming to me," he said. "If you ever change your mind, I'll still be around."

A few months later, in February of 1922, Win was unexpectedly posted to a gunboat in Hong Kong. Wallis took the news quite well. With Win living overseas, no one in Washington would ever guess they were separated. She could live comfortably as a Navy wife whose husband was posted in Asia. Once Win departed, the first thing she wanted to do was start to enjoy life in the city. Through her Navy connections, she soon became immersed in the diplomatic society of Embassy Row, and became a regular on the circuit of cocktail parties, luncheons, and white-tie dinners. Her social skills were improving, and she had a chance to observe grand methods of entertaining.

She also fell in love. Felipe A. Espil was a handsome and charming diplomat from Argentina who was sophisticated and worldly. Wallis was captivated by the ease in which he moved through international society. Unfortunately for Wallis, he planned to become an ambassador, a career goal that required a substantial financial commitment. With no money of his own, he admitted to Wallis he had little choice but to marry an heiress. A middle-class, Navy wife who was still married to her first husband did not fit into his carefully laid plans for the future.

Nearly two years after Win left for Hong Kong, Wallis's mother expressed concern about Wallis's marital uncertainty. Alice felt Wallis should either go through with the divorce and focus on finding another suitable husband or she should return to Win. She couldn't live in limbo forever partying the nights away. Wallis knew her mother was right, but she was confused. She had been so sure divorce was the answer, but Win's absence had given her pause. And the letters he was sending her from Hong Kong were filled with professions of love and affection.

Wallis wanted to get away from Washington to clear her mind, so when Corinne invited her on a tour of Europe, she jumped at the chance. She had never traveled abroad before and the trip sounded like just what she needed. She begged Solomon for the money to travel. He agreed on the condition that she reconsider her separation from Win.

The trip with Corinne lasted six months, and it gave Wallis the time she needed to confront reality. She finally understood her family's concern for her. If she went through with the divorce, she would be left with nowhere to live besides her mother's house, and nothing to look forward to in the future. Win desperately wanted her to join him in Hong Kong, so when she returned to the States, she wrote to him telling him she would arrive later that summer.

On July 17, 1924, Wallis boarded a Navy cargo vessel, *USS Chaumont,* in Norfolk, Virginia for the long journey across the Pacific. She spent her time aboard the *Chaumont* with a group of other military families traveling to their new homes. The ship stopped in Panama where Wallis had to disembark for two days due to severe seasickness. The voyage continued on to Honolulu, Guam, and then the Philippines, where she switched to the *Empress of Canada* for the last leg of the journey.

Wallis would later recall the beauty of Hong Kong's harbor, and how she was filled with such hope the day she arrived. Win was waiting for her at the dock, tanned, handsome, and in excellent health. But their second honeymoon on the other side of the world lasted only two weeks before evidence of Win's drinking began to show itself again. He opened her letters from home, accused her of having numerous affairs, and stopped returning to their apartment at night. He also began to be cruel to her in public, even forcing her to accompany him to nightclubs so he could fawn over the local girls in front of her. Desperately unhappy, with any hope she had of salvaging the marriage destroyed, Wallis located a United States Court for China in

Shanghai where she could file for a divorce. Now that she was far away from the protestations of her family, she was eager to get it over with once and for all.

When she arrived in Shanghai, she moved into the Palace Hotel where she befriended other Navy wives who were waiting for their husbands to return from duty. Being alone in the city was a welcome reprieve from the drama with Win, and she decided she might as well try to enjoy herself. She attended garden parties, dances, and events at the Shanghai Race Club, while she waited for the court to process her file. But the divorce process in Shanghai turned out to be riddled with complications, forcing her to once again put the process on hold.

Discouraged, she decided to take a trip to see the sites of the Forbidden City in Beijing. After a rough boat ride and a harrowing experience on a train where the constant threat of robbers lurked in her mind, she finally arrived and checked into the Grand Hotel de Pekin. A few days later, Wallis ran into Katherine Rogers, a good friend of hers from San Diego. Katherine's first husband had been killed in the war, and her second husband, Herman, was a wealthy New Yorker who was in China to write a book. They offered their guest accommodations to Wallis so that Katherine would have a friend during the day while Herman was writing.

Wallis spent the rest of the year with them, enjoying

her time as a tourist, supplementing her income with nightly poker games, going to the Polo Club, and spending weekends in the countryside where the Rogers owned a small retreat. By the summer of 1925, despite her love of the Orient and her feeling of total relaxation, Wallis knew it was time she returned to the States to move forward with her life. She had been in China for almost one year when she finally booked passage on a ship leaving from Japan and heading to Seattle. Wallis later called her year in China "the most delightful, the most carefree, the most lyric interval of my youth."

On her Pacific crossing, she became violently ill, and the ship's doctor recommended hospitalization as soon as they reached port. Alone and very sick, she had to endure a minor operation in Seattle before she could book a train to Washington, D.C. Win also happened to be in the States on leave. When he heard she was ill, he met her train when it stopped in Chicago and stayed with her until they reached her mother's apartment. It was there she and Win said goodbye forever. She never saw him again.

Despite their tumultuous relationship, Win would speak of her with kindness years later during the abdication crisis. "She is most attractive and has one of the strongest characters I have ever known any person to possess," he told the press. He gallantly refused to comment any further on Wallis or her relationship with the king.

⚜

BACK IN WASHINGTON, D.C., WALLIS BEGAN TO consider her future as she recovered from her illness at her mother's home. She was still young. There was a good chance she could fall in love again and marry someone wonderful who would appreciate and support her. Even her mother had recently remarried for the third time. But there was still the matter of her divorce. She vowed to file for one as soon as her health improved.

Several months later, Wallis stood alone on the train station platform in the sleepy town of Warrenton, Virginia. If she proved twelve months of residency in Virginia, her divorce from Win would be finalized. She chose Warrenton for the simple reason that it was inexpensive.

Wallis remembered the day was hot and dusty, and she felt horribly overdressed in her chiffon dress and high heels. A porter from the Warren Green Hotel arrived to help her with her bags, and Wallis followed him up the small hill toward the main street, the locals turning to stare at her as she passed by. Her room at the hotel was small, only twelve by fifteen feet with ugly worn furniture, faded wallpaper, and a shared bathroom. The one saving grace was a covered porch on the second floor where she could sit and read to pass the time.

Every day, she dined in the small hotel restaurant and watched the traveling salesmen, many of whom were friendly to her. Eventually, she reacquainted with an old friend from Baltimore who was living in the area, and he introduced her to some of the residents of nearby horse country. She also made trips to Washington to visit her mother and to New York City to stay with her friend from Oldfields, Mary Kirk, and Mary's husband, Jacques.

It was in New York one weekend that Mary and Jacques brought Wallis along with them to have dinner at the residence of Ernest and Dorothea Simpson. Ernest impressed Wallis immediately. Although he had been born in New York City, his father was British, and Ernest was a British subject. Wallis was attracted to his passion for travel, his success in the shipping business, and his intelligence. She described him as "reserved in manner, yet with a gift of quiet wit, always well-dressed, a good dancer, fond of the theatre, and obviously well-read." Like Wallis, he was also on the verge of a divorce.

When she wasn't traveling or socializing, her long days alone in Warrenton made her face the looming reality that soon she would have to find a way to support herself unless she remarried. With Ernest Simpson in the back of her mind, she began to consider what type of job she would be interested in doing in case she did not find a husband to support her.

She applied to a fashion magazine by entering a contest, but she was rejected. She considered sales for a department store but did not think she was qualified enough. A friend's husband even tried to help her get a job selling steel for his company in Pittsburgh until they realized she was not mathematically inclined and would never be able to grasp the complex sales calculations required of her on the job. She looked into secretarial courses, but she felt that at age thirty, she was too old to embark on a career as a junior secretary. She was confused, disappointed by her station in life, and unsure of where to live or what to do. A friend recommended she visit a psychic to help lift her spirits. Days later, on her way to an interview with a dress designer, Wallis abruptly cancelled the interview and booked the appointment with the psychic instead.

The psychic told her a startling prophecy. "You will have two more marriages in your life. In middle life, you will exercise considerable power of some kind." Intrigued, Wallis asked her what kind of power she would someday wield.

"The aura is not clear," the psychic replied. "But the power will be considerable. You will become a famous woman."

Wallis asked her if the power would be connected with a job.

"Oh no. Absolutely not. There is nothing to suggest an association with a business career. The indications are all strongly in the opposite direction. You will lead a woman's life, marrying, divorcing, and marrying again with several serious emotional crises. The power that is to come to you will be related to a man."

Wallis was perplexed by the psychic's words, but she shrugged the episode off as mere entertainment. She headed to Penn Station in New York City to catch the train to Warrenton, but she couldn't help wondering if Ernest Simpson, whom she had seen several times while she was in New York, might be part of her future after all.

❧

IN THE SUMMER OF 1927, WALLIS LEFT WARRENTON temporarily to accompany her Aunt Bessie on a tour of Europe. After Aunt Bessie returned home, Wallis remained in Paris, and it was there she received word from her mother that Solomon had died. Wallis left for Baltimore on the next available ocean liner, but she still arrived too late to attend his funeral. At the reading of his will, Solomon, who had never gotten over Wallis's decision to divorce Win, bequeathed the majority of his estate to set up a foundation to provide a home for "impoverished women of gentle birth." Any lingering hope Wallis had for financial independence was dashed when she inherited only a small trust that would terminate in the event she remarried.

Wallis returned to her tiny room at the Warren Green Hotel with mixed emotions. On December 10, 1927, her marriage to Win was finally dissolved by the Fauquier County Court of Virginia. While it meant freedom for her, it also meant the end of her paychecks from the Navy. With nowhere else to go and no immediate plan for the future, Wallis decided to stay on temporarily at the Warren Green Hotel.

It was soon thereafter that Ernest Simpson proposed marriage. He was already divorced from Dorothea, and he was getting ready to move to London to manage the British branch of the family shipping business, Simpson & Simpson. He wanted Wallis to join him in London where they could both start over together.

Wallis considered his proposal for several months. In the spring, she headed back to France to stay with Katherine and Herman Rogers on the Côte d'Azur. While she was there, she contemplated her other options if she didn't marry Ernest. Her attempts to find work had failed. She did not have any other solid prospects for a second marriage, and she was lonely. She was also tired of worrying about her finances as she no longer had Solomon to fall back on. At the end of May, she wrote to Ernest and accepted his proposal of marriage.

Unlike her first wedding, her wedding to Ernest was a simple affair. Ernest handled all the details with the exception of her yellow dress that she ordered from a dressmaker in Paris. On July 21, 1928, they made their way to the Chelsea Registry of Marriages office in London. Wallis recalled it "was more appropriate for a trial than for the culmination of a romance." At eleven o'clock in the morning, Wallis officially became Mrs. Ernest Simpson. The only guests in attendance were Ernest's father and nephew, and their reception was a small champagne breakfast at the Grosvenor Hotel. After breakfast, they headed to Paris where they would start their honeymoon in France and Spain.

Their new lives together began brightly, despite Wallis's homesickness for the States, and the cold, dreary London weather. Her marriage offered her a profound sense of relief. She no longer had to worry about supporting herself or being stigmatized for her divorce. And compared to her volatile relationship with Win, she considered Ernest "regular in his habits, with a temperament as steady and dependable as the trade winds." Her living situation had also improved drastically. They rented a furnished townhouse at 12 Upper Berkeley Street, which she found colossal compared to her room at the Warren Green Hotel and the small government houses she had lived in with Win.

In the early months of their marriage, Wallis tried to adapt to English formalities, and also returned to her habit of reading all the local newspapers and perfecting her homemaking skills. She started creating her own menus and she began to collect antiques and learn more about interior design. Wallis ran her household on a strict budget and carefully managed the allowance she received from her Ernest. By the time they moved into what was to be their permanent home at Number 5 Bryanston Court near Hyde Park, she had learned how to create a lovely, comfortable environment for entertaining, and she began to host cocktail and dinner parties for her new friends.

After almost a year of living in London, Wallis received word from Aunt Bessie that her mother had suffered a stroke and was dying. Ernest and Wallis booked passage immediately on an ocean liner bound for New York City. They traveled by train to Washington and their visit marked the first and only time Alice would meet Ernest. Alice asked Ernest to take good care of her only child, and she told him how happy she was because Wallis had finally settled down in a good marriage.

Ernest returned to London after a week, leaving Wallis behind to keep her mother company. When her condition stabilized, Wallis, feeling torn between her mother and her new responsibilities with Ernest, decided to head back to London figuring there would still be time for a quick Atlantic crossing should Alice's condition grow worse. She bade her mother farewell and promised they would see each other again soon. It would be the last time they spoke. A few months later, Alice slipped into a coma and died on November 2, 1929. Wallis did not make it back to Washington in time to say goodbye.

The death of her mother severed Wallis's last link to the United States. After the funeral, she returned to London with a new outlook. London was her home now, and she was more determined than ever to fit in. She had noticed that one of the habits Londoners had in common was to discuss the happenings of the royal family. Everyone kept up with their existence by reading the Court Circular column in the newspaper. Wallis soon began to follow their daily activities and gossip with interest. She especially liked the Prince of Wales. She had heard he had become a bit of a debonair over the years, and she even jokingly vowed to meet him one day. Ernest's sister, Maud, had met him and took credit for his introduction years before to Freda Dudley Ward.

One winter evening, Wallis was driving to pick Ernest up at the office. There was traffic near St. James Palace, and a crowd had gathered at the main gate. She looked out her car window to see the source of the commotion, knowing it was someone from the royal family. A car pulled out of the drive and sitting in the back seat was the Prince of Wales, staring straight ahead, concern etched on a face she remembered as "boyish." He had just returned from East Africa, recalled from a safari because his father had taken ill.

Wallis watched as the car pulled away, never imagining for a moment what her future beheld.

❧

A YEAR PASSED AFTER WALLIS GLIMPSED THE PRINCE in his car outside the palace. By then, she had settled into a comfortable routine of shopping during the day and entertaining new friends from the American expatriate community in the evening. One such friend was Benjamin Thaw, who was First Secretary of the United States Embassy in London. Benjamin's wife, Connie, was the sister of Thelma Furness, the Prince of Wales's latest girlfriend.

In early January 1931, Connie phoned Wallis at home with an interesting request. Thelma was having a party at her country home, and she had invited Benjamin and Connie, but Connie had a trip to Paris planned already. Connie asked if Wallis and Ernest would mind accompanying Benjamin in her place. The Prince of Wales would be in attendance.

Wallis was excited, but she hesitated. Even though she wanted to meet the prince, she was suddenly nervous by the prospect of seeing him in person. She and Ernest did not hunt, they knew nothing of the customs required for an aristocratic country weekend, and she certainly had no idea how to behave in the presence of royalty.

"Don't be silly," Connie told her. "There'll be no difficulty with the prince. He doesn't stand on ceremony, he isn't stuffy, and besides, he likes Americans."

Wallis still demurred. "Oh Connie, I just can't," she replied.

Connie insisted that Wallis at least ask Ernest if he wanted to go. Ernest was thrilled by the chance to meet the prince and insisted they accept the invitation.

So it was, on a dreary, rainy weekend, Wallis and Ernest left London by train with Benjamin Thaw and headed for the countryside. Wallis had carefully selected a blue-gray Molyneux dress she had bought in Paris as the outfit she would wear to meet members of the royal family. She was still apprehensive on the train, and her anxiety was made worse because she was suffering from a horrible cold. Aside from letting the prince lead every conversation and having to follow his choices in terms of entertainment, she would also have to curtsey to him. Benjamin spent the train ride trying to teach her how to do it.

They arrived at the estate and waited for hours with the other guests over tea until they finally heard voices in the hall. Thelma escorted the Prince of Wales and Prince George into the dining room. Wallis noticed the Prince of Wales was smaller than he appeared in pictures, but just as handsome. Thelma introduced the

Simpsons to him, and Wallis managed to curtsey without slipping. As they had expected, Wallis and Ernest felt slightly out of place in the crowd as the dinner conversation mostly revolved around hounds and hunting. After dinner, everyone broke into smaller groups to play poker and bridge.

Wallis did not have an opportunity to speak to the prince again until the next day when she was seated beside him at the lunch table. The usually outspoken Wallis was nervous again, and her cold was making her miserable. The prince led the conversation, which he later recalled had been about homes in America having central heating. Wallis found him exceedingly polite with a gift for making everyone around him feel at ease, despite the formality that surrounded his position. When the weekend ended, Wallis, Ernest, and Benjamin rode the train back to the city together.

"Do you suppose he will ever marry?" Wallis asked Benjamin. "It seems too bad he doesn't have someone with whom to share these duties."

"Perhaps he might marry some time," Benjamin replied. "He has been in love with several women. There are various stories. But nothing ever comes of these situations. I rather doubt he'll ever marry now, having waited so long."

Wallis had also noticed something else about the prince that she did not share with Ernest or Benjamin. She found him to be hiding an inner sadness or loneliness underneath the graciousness and courtly manners he put on for everyone. She had enjoyed meeting him, and she doubted they would ever cross paths again. She assumed "a woman with the sniffles and a croaking voice would scarcely be judged a desirable addition to the bright company that revolved around the Prince of Wales."

❧ 4 ❧

THE KING & MRS. SIMPSON

I n the summer of 1931, Wallis agreed to be presented to the royal court as was customary for ladies of society. Her new British friends had been urging her to do it, and they even lent her a white satin gown, a feathered headdress, a fan, and a train since expense of a gown and adornments had always been a deterrent for her.

The Prince of Wales and other members of the royal family were there to witness the ceremony. King George and Queen Mary were seated on their thrones, while the prince stood behind them watching each lady curtsey to his parents. When it was Wallis's turn, the prince eyed her with intrigue, "struck," as he later wrote, "by the grace of her carriage and the natural dignity of her movements."

As she moved away, the prince leaned over to speak

to his uncle, the Duke of Connaught, who was standing beside him. "Uncle Arthur," he murmured in a voice louder than he realized, "something ought to be done about the lights. They make all the women look ghastly."

After the ceremony, Thelma invited the Simpsons to attend a party at her London residence. The prince was there too, and he spotted Wallis across the room. He made his way past the other guests to speak with her. When he complimented her dress, she couldn't help but contradict him. "But, Sir," she said, "I understood you thought all the women looked ghastly."

The prince was taken aback by her forthrightness until he realized she was only teasing him. "I had no idea my voice carried so far," he said. He smiled. He liked the American woman who was not afraid to casually joke with him. No one else ever dared to.

When the party ended, Wallis and Ernest happened upon the prince outside as they were leaving. The prince offered them a ride home in his chauffeur-driven car. The Simpsons accepted and they invited the prince up to their flat for a cocktail. He declined, saying it was too late as he wanted to return to the Fort. "I'd like very much to see your flat one day," he said. "I'm told it's charming and seeing it might give me some ideas for brightening up the Fort. But I have to be up so early. Still, if you would be so kind as to invite me again, I'd like to do so."

Wallis and Ernest naturally figured the prince was just being polite. Yet, it was the moment in time that Wallis would later attribute as the beginning of their romance that would cost him his throne.

SHORTLY AFTER WALLIS'S PRESENTATION AT COURT, Thelma and the prince began to include Wallis and Ernest frequently on their party guest lists. Thelma and Wallis were becoming close friends, and the prince was taken with Wallis as well. He found her exceptionally well-informed about current events and genuinely interested in everything from politics to literature and the arts. He was also impressed by her natural gift as a conversationalist and her knowledge of cooking and entertaining. "But most of all," he wrote, "I admired her forthrightness. If she disagreed with some point under discussion, she never failed to advance her own views with vigor and spirit. That side of her enchanted me. A man in my position seldom encountered that trait in other people."

As their friendship deepened, the prince started dropping by the Simpsons' apartment for cocktails in the early evening. At first, Ernest was always present too, but as Wallis and the prince's conversations began lingering later into the nights, Ernest got into the habit of excusing himself so he could focus on business matters in his office.

Wallis was a different type of friend for the prince because she spoke frankly with him and treated him with both normalcy and respect for his position. She asked him endless questions about his ideas and the issues facing Great Britain. One evening, when they were dancing together at a party at the Dorchester Hotel, he famously told her with great regard, "Wallis, you're the only woman who's ever been interested in my job."

By 1934, Wallis and Ernest had become regular fixtures in the prince's life. They were often invited to the Fort and to join him for parties in London and outings to the theatre and nightclubs. The prince especially loved having Wallis as his guest at the Fort. Since she enjoyed decorating, she began to suggest ways to economize and improve his housekeeping and staffing needs. She even made him eggs in his kitchen.

At first, no one in their social set seemed interested in the special affinity the prince had for Wallis. Even Ernest acted as though he and Wallis had simply "adopted" the prince. It was not until Thelma took an extended trip to the United States did their friends realize Wallis was evidently the current object of the prince's affection. Wallis, however, was the only one who did not believe their relationship was anything more than a great friendship.

When Thelma returned from her trip abroad, the prince was politely cool to her. Thelma couldn't help but notice his new fixation with Wallis. Thelma confronted Wallis at Wallis's apartment and demanded to know what was going on between them. She asked if the prince was "keen" on Wallis now instead of her.

"I think he likes me," Wallis responded. "He may be fond of me. But, if you mean by 'keen' that he is in love with me, the answer is definitely no."

Shortly thereafter, Thelma found herself removed from the guest list at the Fort, and she ceased to be a member of the prince's inner circle.

FOR THE SUMMER HOLIDAY OF 1934, THE PRINCE invited Wallis, Ernest, and Aunt Bessie to join him in Biarritz, France where he had rented a villa for the month of August. Ernest declined the invitation because he was traveling to the United States on business, but Wallis, Aunt Bessie, and five others set out for France on the first of August.

The days passed slowly in the villa by the sea where there was nothing to do but swim, sunbathe, and play golf. Later, both the prince and Wallis acknowledged it was in Biarritz, far away from pressures of London, that their mutual feelings deepened. Some nights, just the two of them dined alone in town. But it was not until they were on the open sea on an eleven-day cruise aboard a friend's yacht, *Rosaura*, that something changed between them.

Wallis later wrote, "Perhaps it was during these evenings off the Spanish coast that we crossed the line that marks the indefinable boundary between friend-ship and love. Perhaps it was one evening strolling on the beach at Formentor in Majorca. How can a woman ever really know? How can she ever really tell?"

When they stopped in Cannes to visit Katherine and Herman Rogers, the prince gave Wallis the first of the many jewels he would bestow upon her. Without a word, he handed her a diamond and emerald charm to wear on her bracelet.

After Cannes, they visited Lake Como and Lake Maggiore in Italy before taking the Orient Express to Paris. When they arrived in Paris, the prince bade the group farewell and departed for London. Wallis and Aunt Bessie remained behind to spend some time shopping.

When their trip was over, Wallis and Aunt Bessie boarded the ocean liner *Manhattan* at the French port of Le Havre. Wallis was to sail only as far as Southampton, while Aunt Bessie would continue on to New York.

Aunt Bessie had yet to comment on Wallis's blossoming relationship with the prince, but she had taken notice of it. She waited until they were having dinner on their last night before broaching the topic.

"Wallis, isn't the prince rather taken with you?" she asked.

"Whatever makes you think that?" Wallis replied. She had been dreading confronting the situation aloud. But she knew her aunt would never have asked the question if she did not have cause for concern.

"These eyes aren't so old that they can't see what is in his every glance."

Wallis struggled to respond. A part of her still believed the prince's interest in her would fade. She wanted to revel in it as a fairy tale or a dream without consequences.

"Isn't all this very dangerous for you?" Aunt Bessie pressed. "If you let yourself enjoy this kind of life, it will make you very restless and dissatisfied with everything you've ever known before. I see no happy outcome to such a situation."

Wallis denied there was anything more than a close friendship between them, but Aunt Bessie's questions resonated with her. She herself did not quite understand why the prince had fallen for her of all people. But she knew what attracted her to him. "He possessed an unmistakable aura of power and authority," she wrote. "His slightest wish seemed always to be translated instantly into the most impressive kind of reality. Trains were held; yachts materialized; the best suites in the finest hotels were flung open; aeroplanes stood waiting...it seemed unbelievable that I, Wallis Warfield of Baltimore, Maryland could be part of this enchanted world."

ERNEST WAS WAITING FOR WALLIS WHEN THE OCEAN liner docked in Southampton. At first, he had been flattered by the prince's attention to Wallis, but now he was suspicious that what had begun as a friendship had turned into a childlike infatuation on the part of the prince. Despite his deep regard for the monarchy, he was growing tired of the prince's monopoly over Wallis. He accepted the prince had been bowled over by his wife, but he was unsure of what to do about it. As soon as Wallis disembarked, he immediately peppered her with questions about the trip.

"I can't describe it," Wallis told him. "All I can say is that it was like being Wallis in Wonderland."

Ernest looked at her with irritation. "It sounds to me indeed like a trip behind the 'Looking Glass.' Or, better yet, an excursion into the realm of Peter Pan's Never-Never Land."

ONE AFTERNOON, SEVERAL MONTHS AFTER THE TRIP to Biarritz, the prince was late returning to the Fort. His guests, including Wallis, were already there waiting for him. He had been at Balmoral Castle, where the royal family had congregated after the launch of the new British ocean liner, *Queen Mary,* that had been named in honor of his mother.

"I have a little surprise for you," the prince whispered to Wallis when he arrived. After dinner, he disappeared from the table. The guests could hear the sound of bagpipes playing, and the prince reappeared followed by another musician. They stopped at the entrance to the dining room, paused for a moment, and then began to play a haunting song no one in the room had heard before.

One of the guests spoke up when they finished. "Sir, I thought I knew my pipe tunes, but I can't place that one. I don't know where you found it, but I must say it is delightful."

"As a matter of fact, I wrote it myself. It's called *Majorca*," the prince said, and he looked at Wallis pointedly.

۞

BY THE WINTER OF 1935, WALLIS'S RELATIONSHIP with the prince had finally taken its toll on Ernest. When the prince invited them to join him on a ski trip to Austria in February, Ernest angrily refused to go, once again telling Wallis he had to travel to the States on business. He asked Wallis if she planned to go to Austria without him.

"Of course," she replied. "Why not? I wouldn't dream of missing it."

"I rather thought we might have gone to New York together," Ernest said. "I see now I was wrong."

He stood up and slammed the door to his room, leaving Wallis alone at the dinner table. She knew she ought to decline the prince's invitation, but as much as she still cared for Ernest, she was also slowly admitting to herself that she was falling in love with the prince. And she knew there was nothing she could do to stop it from happening, even if it meant risking her marriage.

IN EARLY FEBRUARY, WALLIS, THE PRINCE, AND A group of friends left for Kitzbuehel where they checked into the Grand Hotel. The men skied all day, while the women met them later for dinner and dancing. It was another whirlwind vacation for Wallis. There was no question the prince knew how to enjoy himself. On a whim, the entire party went to Vienna because the prince felt like waltzing, and then on another whim, they went to Budapest to listen to the music of the gypsies.

As Aunt Bessie predicted, the more Wallis stepped into the charmed and cloistered world of the prince, the more difficult it became for her to muster up interest in her old life. Yet she was still convinced the prince would soon find another favorite companion, and she would be back in her flat with Ernest living her simple, uncomplicated life.

MEANWHILE, IN LONDON, NEWS OF THE PRINCE'S relationship with Wallis was slowly becoming the latest gossip amongst the upper class. Wallis suddenly found herself the toast of the town, and she and Ernest were flooded with invitations to society parties. As a faithful subject of the Crown, Ernest continued to attend city events and weekends at the Fort with Wallis, but their marriage was already irreparably damaged, and silence surrounded them at home. Making matters worse, Ernest's shipping business was encountering financial trouble due to the Great Depression. Wallis knew they needed to restrict their budget and even put their flat on the market, but the luxurious world she frequented made it easy for her to push thoughts about finances to the back of her mind.

In May of 1935, the prince invited Wallis and Ernest to the State Ball to celebrate King George and Queen Mary's Silver Jubilee, marking their 25th year of reign. His parents were all too aware of the presence of a "Mrs. Simpson" in their son's life, and they were not pleased about it.

Wallis felt the king's eyes on her as she danced with the prince. She remembered, "Something in his look made me feel that all this graciousness and pageantry were but the glittering tip of an iceberg that extended down into unseen depths I could never plumb, depths filled with an icy menace for such as me."

Just eight months later, the prince and Wallis were relaxing at the Fort when a messenger rushed in and delivered a note to the prince. The prince immediately shared it with Wallis. King George had taken ill and the royal family feared the end was near. Shaken, the prince ordered his airplane to standby and he left at once for the Sandringham Estate in Norfolk.

At midnight on January 20, 1936, the royal family stood in sorrow at the bedside of King George V. The prince realized his father had passed away and he was now king when his mother reached for his hand and brought it to her lips. His younger brother, Prince George, repeated her gesture. He later wrote the gestures embarrassed him. "I could not bring myself to believe that the members of my own family, or indeed anyone else, should be expected to humble themselves before me in this way."

The prince, now King Edward VIII, was overcome by a profound mixture of grief and apprehension. He grieved for the loss of his father, and he was equally concerned by the enormous task now before him. He also felt utterly and horribly alone. He was forty-one years old and king of an empire that spanned the globe.

The next day he returned to London on an airplane. It was symbolic of what was to come with the new reign as no British monarch had ever before flown in an aircraft.

He faced the Privy Councilors in St. James's Palace so he could receive the proclamation of accession to the throne.

"We...do now hereby...publish and proclaim, That the High and Mighty Prince Edward Albert Christian George Andrew Patrick David, is now, by the Death of our late Sovereign of Happy Memory, become our lawful and rightful Liege, Lord Edward the Eighth, by the Grace of God, of Great Britain, Ireland, and the British Dominions beyond the Seas, King, Defender of the Faith, Emperor of India."

Also in London, at Number 10 Downing Street, was Stanley Baldwin, the conservative prime minister. He called for a meeting with Duff Cooper, the Secretary of State for War. Baldwin asked Cooper for more details about the relationship the king was having with a certain "Mrs. Simpson." He already knew Wallis was an upper-middle class, married American who had already been divorced once, thanks to the Metropolitan Police who had been spying on her for over a year.

The entire situation was cause for alarm as far as Baldwin was concerned because the police reports also lent damaging credence to the depth of the prince's attachment to her. He did not care if Mrs. Simpson was the king's mistress, but something about her influence on him indicated that it was more than just a casual affair. Baldwin was especially troubled that the law stated that any woman the king married would automatically become queen, and any children of their union would be successors to the throne.

"If she were what I would call a respectable whore, I wouldn't mind," he told Duff. But what if the king decided to marry her? The idea of Wallis as queen was appalling to him. In no way was this "Mrs. Simpson" a suitable match for the new king.

THE SECOND CEREMONY MARKING HIS ACCESSION WAS a Proclamation by the Heralds. It was filled with such pomp and circumstance that the king was even able to watch the event himself from the window of an apartment at St. James Palace. He invited Wallis to join him.

A photograph taken of them from below shows them looking solemn and apart. Wallis is seated, wearing a hat and fur wrap, and the king is standing to her right, his face drawn and his head resting against the wall. They knew what the change before them meant. His every move, though documented before, would now be chronicled. And his burgeoning love for the married Wallis Simpson could no longer continue privately without judgment or criticism.

As they made their way to the exit later, Wallis turned to him. "How thoughtful of you to bother thinking of me and to ask me here. This has made me realize how different your life is going to be."

He touched her arm. "Wallis, there will be a difference of course. But nothing can ever change my feelings towards you."

The king had already assessed the complications surrounding their romance and he came to the conclusion that the best solution was to marry Wallis. He expected some people would be outraged, especially given the major issue of divorce not being recognized by the Church of England. Most inconveniently, his position as king meant he was the token head of the Church of England.

But he was used to getting his way. He was the king for heaven's sake, and he firmly believed he should be able to marry any woman he wanted. He decided he would just have to settle into his new role and then make his intentions known to the world. There was only one person he believed was truly standing in his way. Wallis needed to divorce Ernest Simpson as soon as possible.

In the meantime, he slowly went about making minor changes to life at Buckingham Palace. He fixed the clocks in the palace to read the exact time as his father had always kept them a confusing thirty minutes fast. He attempted to walk to meetings in London rather than being driven by a chauffeur. He dressed in a more relaxed, fashionable style rather than the stuffy attire of his predecessors. Even his hobbies were regarded as bourgeois. Instead of hosting formal dinner parties, the king preferred golf, gardening, and nightclubs.

A vein of dissent began to flow throughout the British aristocracy as some believed he was behaving too casually for a king. Several members of high society began to wonder if their established custom of living was becoming a facet of the past. There were also members of his staff who had worked for his father for years who were beginning to dislike what they perceived as a modernization of the Court.

A WEEK AFTER HIS FATHER DIED, HE WAS PAID A VISIT by the formidable archbishop of Canterbury. The archbishop, a longtime friend of his father's, was hoping to launch a "Recall to Religion" campaign the following year. Participation in the Church of England had been dropping steadily and the archbishop needed to ensure he could count on the king's support. But the king was not interested in religion, and he was certainly not interested in the archbishop, whom he found to be "medieval." The meeting ended badly.

A few weeks later, another meeting took place. Ernest Simpson requested an audience with the king while Wallis was shopping in Paris. Unbeknownst to her, and fortuitous for the king, Ernest had fallen in love with another woman.

On a visit to New York the previous summer, Ernest had spent time with Mary Kirk Raffray, the very person who had introduced Ernest to Wallis years before. Mary was in the middle of a divorce from her husband, Jacques, and she had always had great affection for Ernest. A love affair had developed between them, and suddenly for Ernest, enough was enough with Wallis. He had been playing the understanding husband for a long time, and he was growing tired of his role as the rejected spouse. He wanted to move on with his life, and he wanted to know what the king's intentions were toward Wallis.

The king told him he planned to marry her. "Do you really think I would be crowned without Wallis at my side?" he asked.

Ernest was stunned. He had gone to see the king to make sure Wallis would be cared for financially if he divorced her. He never expected the king to actually marry Wallis. He had assumed marriage to her was impossible. But the king insisted he would find a way to make it work, and that Ernest and Wallis should divorce as soon as possible. Astonished, Ernest left with the king's assurance that Wallis would never have to worry about money again.

Neither man mentioned the meeting to Wallis. She still believed her presence in the king's life would diminish with time, and she would be left with beautiful memories and the knowledge she had once been loved by a king. Of course, the king had fantasized to her about the day they would marry, but she never expected him to actually propose. She presented too many problems for him. She would not be able to produce an heir to the throne, and if she and Ernest separated then she would be twice divorced. She knew in the eyes of the government, the church, and the royal family, she was not a suitable match for the king. She was also aware she was perceived as too American, too rambunctious, and too middle-class. She simply did not have the pedigree to become Queen Wallis.

Yet, despite the odds against the king and Wallis, the king's meeting with Ernest set into motion the beginning of the end of Wallis and Ernest's marriage. Wallis soon received a telegraph from Mary Kirk

Raffray asking to visit Wallis and Ernest in London for a few months. Wallis agreed and Mary arrived on March 24th.

On March 27th, Wallis, Mary, Ernest, and several other guests spent the weekend at the Fort. The king surprised Wallis with an extravagant diamond and ruby bracelet secretly inscribed with the words: "Hold Tight, 27.iii.36."

A few days after their weekend at the Fort, Ernest also surprised Wallis by announcing his intention to marry Mary. He admitted their affair had begun in New York the previous summer and now they were deeply in love. Wallis was taken aback. Any lingering hope she had of keeping her relationship with the king and her marriage to Ernest intact was now destroyed. Her future had slipped beyond her control. Ernest was leaving her for another woman, and the king was convinced he was going to marry her.

"I was kept in the dark," she wrote to Aunt Bessie. "Isn't it all ridiculous?"

When the king learned Ernest had disclosed his affair with Mary and asked for a divorce, he gifted Wallis with a substantial sum of money for her to live comfortably until their marriage.

Wallis and Ernest remained at Bryanston Court together for appearances' sake until early summer, although Ernest continued to spend his free time with Mary. In May, the king planned his first official dinner party for several of his friends and colleagues, including Duff Cooper, Lady Cunard, Charles Lindbergh, and Stanley Baldwin. Despite Ernest's attendance at the dinner, the king had slyly remarked to Wallis, "Sooner or later my prime minister must meet my future wife." Though Wallis and Baldwin were seated at opposite ends of the table and did not engage in conversation, the momentous occasion did not go unnoticed by the press. The next day, her name appeared in the Court Circular, discreetly marking for the first time that "Mrs. Simpson" was the mistress of the king.

By early June, the king was anxious for Wallis and Ernest's divorce proceedings to begin. He met with Ernest again privately and impressed upon him the need to put their plans into action. "My talk with Ernest was difficult this evening, but I must get after him now or he won't move," the king told Wallis.

Later that summer, the king chartered a beautiful yacht called *Nahlin* so he and Wallis could explore the Aegean Sea and the Dalmatian Coast. Crowds gathered in every port of call to welcome the famous king and catch a glimpse of Wallis. In Dubrovnik, the crowds chanted, "Long live love." And, one evening, as they were anchored off Cetinje, peasants lined the shore singing for them and waving flaming torches in the darkness.

"I suppose you think this for me," the king said to Wallis.

"Of course. Who else would it be for?"

"It is all for you because they believe a king is in love with you."

Then a photograph was taken that caught them off-guard. The king was starting to climb out of *Nahlin's* launch boat when Wallis put her hand on his wrist. Unbeknownst to them, the picture was published in newspapers across the world.

When the trip ended, the king returned to England and Wallis went to Paris. She checked into the Hotel Meurice and received her mail that had been forwarded from London. She was shocked to find letters from friends concerned about her well-being, and also ones from Aunt Bessie who had mailed her clippings from newspapers published in the United States. Wallis already knew the press in the States had been covering her affair with the king for several months, but now they had a picture to prove it was true. It seemed their romance was being reported everywhere except in Great Britain where the press was still respecting the king's privacy. And every publication was asking the same question—who was this mysterious Mrs. Simpson?

After Wallis read the clippings, she felt miserable and powerless. She did not believe Great Britain would ever tolerate her marrying the king, and she was becoming increasingly convinced their affair was ruining both of their lives. Sick with a cold and stuck in the hotel, she had time to contemplate the situation. She decided the only way to end the dilemma was to remain with Ernest and break off her relationship with the king. She mailed him a letter saying as much...*I know Ernest and have the deepest affection and respect for him. I feel I am better with him than with you—and so you must understand. I am sure dear David that in a few months your life will run again as it did before and without my nagging...I am sure you and I would only create disaster together.*

But in typical Wallis fashion, she was unable to keep her thoughts to herself when she phoned the king later that same day. The king dismissed her concerns. Even before he received her letter, he wrote one to her that same evening professing his love for her...*Why do you say such hard things to David on the telephone sometimes?...You see I do love you so entirely and in every way Wallis. Madly tenderly adoringly and with admiration and such confidence... Please try and trust me like you love me and don't have any doubts. I promise you there is not the slightest reason to.*

His refusal to accept her hesitation left her with little choice but to trust him that things would work out somehow in the end.

The king wanted them to be married before his coronation on May 12, 1937. When Wallis returned to London, she filed for divorce with Theodore Goddard, the attorney the king had suggested. The king also wanted her to move out of her apartment with Ernest and into more luxurious accommodations, so she rented a furnished house in Regent's Park.

As word of her impending divorce began to circulate in London society, the king was faced with a growing amount of scrutiny from his advisors. He denied having anything to do with Wallis's decision to end her marriage to Ernest. He adamantly maintained that "Mrs. Simpson" was just a close friend. Of course, no one in his inner circle believed him.

Wallis and Ernest's divorce hearing was scheduled for October 27, 1936, in the town of Ipswich on the east coast of England. In early October, Wallis, accompanied by her friends, the Hunters, left London for Ipswich where she had to establish a temporary residence so the divorce could be held in a court there. She rented a house on the beach in Felixstowe, an off-season resort town now devoid of visitors. Wallis and the Hunters took long walks on the beach and tried to relax, but nothing seemed to cure her increasing anxiety over her future with the king. She was hearing disturbing reports from the Hunters that the king's reputation was faltering on her account, and she still feared he would never be able to obtain the necessary approvals to marry her. On October 14, she wrote another letter to the king begging him to tell her if he regretted his decision. Once again, the king insisted it would all work out and she should not worry about a thing.

WHILE WALLIS WAS IN FELIXSTOWE, THE KING requested a meeting with Lord Beaverbrook, his personal friend and the owner of the *Daily Express* newspaper. The king asked Lord Beaverbrook for help in keeping the news of Wallis's divorce out of the British newspapers. He told Lord Beaverbrook that Wallis should not be forced to endure negative publicity simply because she was a friend of the king's. Lord Beaverbrook had heard the rumors of the king's affair with Wallis. He knew the American press had exploded with news of the relationship, but he was sympathetic to the king's plea, and he immediately set out to help silence the other newspapers.

Stanley Baldwin also heard about the impending divorce and requested a private meeting with the king. On October 20, Baldwin drove out to the Fort and the king met him in the drawing room. Baldwin appeared nervous and asked for a whiskey, which surprised the king since it was only ten o'clock in the morning. Baldwin went on to explain what the king already knew. His relationship with Wallis was beginning to cause a public outcry, and the British press had not even mentioned the divorce yet.

The king suspected the true reason for Baldwin's visit was to determine if he planned to marry Wallis after her divorce became final. But for whatever reason, Baldwin never managed to get the words out. Instead, he commented on the Fort's garden and got back in his car.

❧❦❧

WALLIS'S DIVORCE PETITION FROM ERNEST WAS granted on October 27, 1936, on the grounds of Ernest's adultery. She would be able to marry again after a period of six months if she and Ernest behaved appropriately and did nothing to jeopardize the ruling.

The king was relieved when he heard the news. Now he had ample time before his coronation to convince the government to approve his desire to make her his bride.

Meanwhile, across the Atlantic, Aunt Bessie, sensing there was trouble ahead for her niece, set sail for Great Britain on the *Queen Mary*.

❧❦❧

AFTER HER COURT HEARING, WALLIS RETURNED TO London to the comfort of her new home in Cumberland Terrace. The king arrived shortly thereafter for dinner with a surprise planned for Wallis. That evening, he formally proposed marriage with the presentation of a gigantic emerald ring. The inscription inside read: "WE are ours now, 27x36." "WE" was his acronym for "Wallis and Edward."

❧

THE FIRST FEW WEEKS AFTER THEIR PRIVATE engagement were relatively calm. Thanks to Lord Beaverbrook, the British press remained quiet, letting the king busy himself with other matters. He opened Parliament on November 3, and then traveled to the coastal town of Portland to tour the royal fleet. He was met with the usual adulation from the crowds who gathered to greet him, most of whom were unaware the government was starting to react badly to rumors of his engagement.

When he returned to the Fort after his trip, he opened a letter from his assistant, Alex Hardinge. The letter began with Hardinge expressing his duty to report that the government was against his marriage to Wallis. Hardinge had been put up to the task of writing the letter by several government ministers, including Baldwin. His letter went on to state that if the king moved forward with the marriage, the government might resign. Compounding the problem, Hardinge warned, was that the press could no longer respect their agreement to avoid reporting on the king's private affairs.

The king was stunned by how much had happened in so little time. He knew many of his subjects and ministers didn't approve of Wallis, but the letter made the king face the reality that his once-loyal forces were now working together against him.

The king took a long bath and read Hardinge's letter again. He did not believe Hardinge would write such a letter on his own, and he was correct in his assumption that Hardinge had been reporting the king's actions to Baldwin. The king also knew there was no way Hardinge would have been privy to the government's talk of resignation unless someone told him on purpose.

Infuriated, the king did not respond to Hardinge, who had mentioned he was available anytime to discuss matters further. Instead, he contacted his trusted advisor, Walter Monckton. Monckton advised him that a temporary separation from Wallis might settle matters down considerably. They agreed the king's first step should be to speak directly to the prime minister.

Later, the king shared Hardinge's letter with Wallis, who was stunned by its contents. "To use a good American expression, they are about to give me the works," the king told her. "They want me to give you up. I intend to see the prime minister tomorrow. I shall tell him that if the Government is opposed to our marriage, as Alec Hardinge says in his letter, then I am prepared to go."

Wallis was aghast. Giving up his throne was the last thing she wanted. He would lose everything, and she would be blamed by the world for ruining his life. "You must not be impetuous," Wallis implored. "There must be some other way."

The king informed her he had arranged for a

meeting with Baldwin at Buckingham Palace the next day. He also needed to find Lord Beaverbrook, whom he soon learned was aboard an ocean liner en route to New York. The king reached him by way of the ship's telephone and begged him to return to England. Since the boat was already halfway across the Atlantic, Lord Beaverbrook agreed, but his only option was to remain aboard and return on an eastbound ship once he arrived in New York.

THE KING GOT RIGHT TO THE POINT WHEN BALDWIN arrived at Buckingham Palace the following day. "I understand that you and several members of the Cabinet have some fear of a constitutional crisis developing over my friendship with Mrs. Simpson," he said.

"Yes, Sir, that is correct," Baldwin replied.

"I intend to marry Mrs. Simpson as soon as she is free to marry." The king also stated that he would abdicate if the government opposed his choice of a wife.

Baldwin said relatively little during the rest of the meeting. He smoked his pipe and listened to the king explain the reasons for his devotion to Wallis, and why his love for her would never allow him to relegate Wallis's role to that of a mistress.

Baldwin knew that if the king gave up his reign, then the king's quiet, undemanding brother, Prince

Albert, would assume the throne. Albert was a family man, married with two little girls, Princess Elizabeth and Princess Margaret. He was a man more like the late King George. Prince Albert did not captivate the passions of the crowds, he never spoke out of turn, and he did not cause controversy with modern ideas and avant-garde ways. As far as the prime minister was concerned, Prince Albert would be an ideal king.

If Baldwin had a strategy to remove the king from the throne, he never admitted it. But his audience with the king had confirmed exactly what he needed to know —the king was not going to abandon Wallis under any circumstances.

❧

THE LETTER FROM HARDINGE AND THE MEETING with Baldwin were so unsettling, the king began to accept the staggering fact that his days on the throne were numbered unless he gave up Wallis. And since he was not going to break off their engagement, then he had another very important person to face.

At eight-thirty that evening, he arrived in white tie at Marlborough House, Queen Mary's home since her husband had died ten months before. It would be the first time he ever mentioned his relationship with Wallis to his mother.

He waited until the endless dinner finished before

discussing the recent controversy surrounding his personal affairs. He explained to Queen Mary that he loved Wallis dearly and planned to marry her despite the opposition from the prime minister and the government. He insisted that he should have the right to decide whom he could and could not marry. And if the government did not agree with his choice of a wife, then he was prepared to pass his kingship to Prince Albert.

Queen Mary was astonished. She had spent her lifetime in rigid, devoted service to Great Britain. She could not begin to envisage that her eldest son would ever abdicate. Furthermore, she had no desire to see their family's reputation marred over something as trivial as a love affair. She had perhaps long ago stopped hoping her son would settle down and wed a suitable European princess or a member of the British aristocracy. But a forty-year-old woman from America who was about to be twice divorced was another matter. She urged him to consider his decision carefully.

"Please won't you let me bring Wallis Simpson to see you?" he asked. "If you were to meet her, you would understand what she means to me and why I cannot give her up. I have waited a long time to find the person whom I wished to marry."

Much to the king's disappointment, Queen Mary flatly refused his request.

TWO DAYS LATER, THE KING SET OUT BY TRAIN WITH his entourage to tour the depressed steel towns of South Wales. The people were thrilled by his visit. He spoke openly to the press, asserting that the government was not doing its share to help the unemployed workers. His comments only further infuriated his detractors in the government.

When he returned to London, Wallis informed him that one of her friends had suggested over lunch at Claridge's that she and the king marry morganatically. It meant Wallis would be the king's legal wife, but she would not share his rank or be granted a royal title. She would not be queen. She would have no rights over his property and any children they might have would not succeed him. The king frowned at the suggestion. He found it unsuitable for Wallis, but she insisted he at least consider it.

The king mulled it over. "The lesser status, I was sure, would never prevent Wallis with her American charm and energy from fulfilling with undiminished spirit the many duties devolving upon the king's Consort."

He consulted Walter Monckton who agreed it was worth a try. But Monckton also cautioned that complications could arise because the government would have to pass a law to allow the morganatic marriage to take place. Monckton highly doubted they would ever agree to pass the legislation.

They contacted Baldwin who agreed to bring the matter before the Cabinet. The king waited patiently for a response. When one did not arrive in a timely fashion, he sent for Baldwin himself. It turned out Baldwin had not done anything with the request because he doubted it would ever be agreed upon. Still, the king pressed him to move forward with the proposal.

Baldwin then posed the question that he knew would ultimately doom the king. "Sir, would you like me to examine the proposition formally?" he asked.

The king told him to proceed. But by agreeing to put forth a formal request to the British Cabinet and the Dominion Governments regarding his marriage to Wallis, the king had unknowingly placed his throne in a precarious position. By asking the government's permission, he would be forced to adhere to their decision.

The next day, Lord Beaverbrook finally returned from his round-trip across the Atlantic. He arrived at the Fort and listened to the king describe the morganatic proposal with dismay. He, too, doubted it would ever be approved. He urged the king to withdraw it from consideration at once. The king refused. Instead, he requested Lord Beaverbrook's full support. Lord Beaverbrook had little choice but to reluctantly agree.

After lunch, Lord Beaverbrook left for London to try to help in any way he could.

On November 27, Baldwin met with the Cabinet and gave the government and the Dominions two choices—do you recommend the king marry morganatically or do you recommend abdication if he insists upon marrying?

AS NEWS OF THE KING'S CRISIS TRICKLED OUT, THE situation for Wallis in London was becoming dangerous. Angry crowds were gathering on the sidewalk, hate mail started arriving in her mailbox, and the king even received a bomb threat on her house. He ordered Wallis and Aunt Bessie to leave the city at once and take refuge at the Fort.

When they arrived, they were further confronted with the gravity of the situation. They tried to remain calm despite the harried presence of the king's supporters and the telephone ringing off the hook.

IT TOOK SEVERAL DAYS BEFORE WORD CAME IN THAT the government and Dominions had reached a decision. The king left the Fort for Buckingham Palace at once to meet with Baldwin and learn the outcome.

Baldwin delivered the terse news. It was Wallis or his throne.

"So, Mr. Baldwin, you really leave me with one choice," the king said.

"Believe me, Sir," Baldwin replied, "it is my sincere hope—and the hope of the Cabinet—that you will remain our king."

The king repeated his intention. He was still going to marry Wallis.

When the king returned to the Fort that evening, he said nothing to Wallis or Aunt Bessie. His lack of elation was enough for them to guess the government's answer.

After dinner, he asked Wallis to step outside with him for a walk. They only got as far as the terrace. He told her that the morganatic proposal had been denied. Even the Dominions had rejected it. Compounding everything was an announcement from the press stating that given the dire circumstances unfolding for the monarchy, they had no choice but to break the gentleman's agreement that protected the king's private life.

"So, it now comes to this," the king said. "Either I must give you up or abdicate. And I don't intend to give you up."

Wallis was devastated. Abdication, which had once

seemed so impossible, was now looming before them. As much as she loved being the king's favorite companion over the years, she had never wanted to jeopardize his throne.

"David," she said, using their intimate form of address, "I'm going to leave." She suggested France. She could stay with Katherine and Herman Rogers. Their villa, Lou Viei, was secluded on an estate. She knew she would be safe there.

The king sadly agreed with her decision. He had considered her situation already. If she left the country temporarily, she would at least be safe and sheltered from the brewing storm.

The next morning, December 3, 1936, the press exploded with the news, some showing support for the king, others violently opposed to him marrying Wallis. The headlines screamed, "Grave Constitutional Issue," "Grave Crisis," and "Constitutional Crisis."

The king, who had awoken first, planned to hide the newspapers from Wallis, but they had inadvertently been given to her on her breakfast tray. She got dressed and went to find him.

He was in the drawing room working on his radio broadcast, which he believed might be his last chance to salvage his throne. He hugged her when she came in.

"Dearest David," she stammered. "I am so sorry I've done this to you."

❧ 5 ❧

FLIGHT TO FRANCE

December 3, 1936

An hour after Wallis left Fort Belvedere for the night ferry to France, the king jumped into action. He decided to return to Buckingham Palace to meet with the prime minister. He needed Baldwin's approval before he addressed his subjects over the radio.

When he arrived at the palace, Walter Monckton was already there waiting for him. They began to go over the details of the speech again. "*Neither Mrs. Simpson nor I have ever sought to insist that she should be Queen. All we desired was that our married happiness should carry with it a proper title and dignity for her, befitting my wife. Now that I have at last been able to take you into my confidence, I feel it is best to go away for a while so that you may reflect calmly and quietly, but without undue delay, in what I have said. Nothing is nearer to my heart than that I should return; but whatever may befall, I shall always have a deep affection for my country, for the Empire, and for you all."*

He wasn't sure where he would go, but he hoped his absence might spark a cry for his return and an outpouring of acceptance for Wallis. He assumed he still at least had the majority of the general public on his side.

Baldwin was not amused nor interested in the idea of a radio broadcast. He agreed to consult the Cabinet at a meeting the next day, but he made no promises to the king that his request would be honored.

After the prime minister left, the king called for his lawyer, George Allen, and Walter Monckton. He informed the men that he wanted his two closest allies, Lord Beaverbrook and Winston Churchill, to review his radio draft. He knew Lord Beaverbrook and Churchill supported his marriage to Wallis, and that they also thought abdicating was a ludicrous plan. The king hoped they might be able to use their widespread influence to sway public and government sentiment. He asked Monckton and Allen to personally deliver the speech to them. He had somewhere else he needed to go. Earlier that morning, he had received a distressing message that only added to his anxiety. Queen Mary had asked him to report to her at Marlborough House.

He arrived there to find the queen distraught. She was upset because he had not been to visit her in ten days and he still had not informed her of his plans regarding Wallis. She could not fathom that he had not come to his senses, and that he was still contemplating giving up his position, his birthright, and his country for a woman. The king listened to her, but he could not tell her the one thing she wanted to hear. He was not going to abandon Wallis.

As his chauffeur brought him back to Buckingham Palace, he noticed a crowd had gathered outside the front gates near the statue of Queen Victoria. She had also somewhat abandoned her country for love. When her beloved husband, Albert, died, the middle-aged queen was devastated and all but withdrew from public affairs, living the rest of her life a recluse. It was because of her absence that the ruling party was passed from monarch to Parliament. Never again would a British king or queen exert any definitive influence over government affairs.

Looking at the gates looming before him, the king was suddenly filled with a loathing for the palace. He wondered if he belonged there at all. "The answer came immediately—certainly not alone," he thought.

IT WAS STILL RAINING AS WALLIS'S CAR RACED SOUTH through the back roads of England toward the southern coast. The windows were covered in steam, and the party rode in silence to the boat that would take her away.

Beside her in the back seat, Lord Brownlow was growing anxious. He still needed to hatch his secret plan. The night before, he met with some other friends of the king, including Lord Beaverbrook, Walter Monckton, and George Allen. They all came to the conclusion that because the king had already proposed to Wallis, he would never call off the marriage being as he was a dignified gentleman. And besides, the king had been the one who had pressured her to divorce Ernest. The group reasoned that it was up to Wallis to renounce him instead. It did not need to be a permanent renunciation—they only needed to postpone their marriage until things settled down. The men decided Lord Brownlow had the best chance of convincing her to do so, since he was a lord-in-waiting to the king and would be able visit with Wallis at the Fort.

Lord Brownlow had been trying to concoct an opportunity to meet with her when the king suddenly telephoned him and asked him to accompany Wallis to France. Lord Brownlow couldn't believe the lucky twist of fate.

In the car, he waited nervously for the right moment to tell Wallis of their scheme.

AFTER A SUFFICIENT AMOUNT OF DRIVING HAD TAKEN place, Lord Brownlow gently asked Wallis what made her leave the country so suddenly.

In her frantic state of mind, she told him she was leaving the king forever. "I have only one desire now," she said. "It is to go just as far away as I can, just as fast as I can—to finish it."

Lord Brownlow was dumbfounded. That was not the answer he had anticipated. He expected her to say the king was sending her to France out of fear for her safety. Instead, Wallis seemed to be on their side in believing the king should stay on his throne. Why were they going anywhere then? He told the driver to stop the car.

He proposed she stay at his house in Belton, England. If she was giving up the king, then she did not need to be in France to do it.

No, Wallis replied. The farther away from the king the better.

Lord Brownlow spoke carefully in hushed tones. "What I am getting at is simply this. With you gone, the king will not stay in England."

"He will stay. He has to stay. They will never let him go."

"That is where you are wrong. The king himself told me that his mind is made up. He intends to leave the country unless and until the Government gives way...I can see only one outcome—abdication."

Wallis continued to insist the only way to truly remove herself from the king's life was to go to France. "You must remember," Wallis said, "that until this morning I was an utter stranger to all but a handful of people in Great Britain. There is no one to speak up for me. I am sure there is only one solution—that is for me to remove myself from the king's life. That is what I am doing now."

Lord Brownlow knew better, but frustrated and defeated, he reverted to being an English gentleman and told the chauffeur to drive on.

❧

THE PARTY ARRIVED AT THE FERRY AS PLANNED, concealed by darkness. No one took any special notice of a driver dropping off what appeared to be an ordinary middle-aged couple and one of their servants. Wallis wanted to telephone the king from the pier, but the poor weather had delayed their drive and they were out of time.

Wallis and Lord Brownlow checked in under the alias "Mr. and Mrs. Harris," and were led to their reserved cabins on the boat. The king's chauffeur, Ladbrook, was already onboard waiting for them. He assured them Wallis's Buick was discreetly stowed in the ship's hold.

As the ferry crew readied themselves for departure,

the English Channel stretched out before them infinitely, a forbidding blend of blackness and fog. In those final moments as the ferry pulled away from the dock, Wallis believed she might never again return to England.

❧

WHEN THE FERRY ARRIVED IN DIEPPE, FRANCE, IT was after midnight on December 4. Wallis let Ladbrook and Lord Brownlow disembark ahead of her to handle the customs officials. They returned shaken. In their haste to leave England, they had forgotten to change the registration papers of Wallis's car. The French authorities were now well aware that "Mrs. Harris" was actually the King of England's notorious Mrs. Simpson. It was only a matter of time before the press would know as well.

They had no choice but to move in the direction of Cannes. Lord Brownlow had already chosen Rouen, a town located forty miles inland, as the place where they would spend the night. The group piled into her Buick and set out for the historic port on the Seine.

Amidst the medieval buildings, they located a small hotel called the Hotel de la Poste. It was after two o'clock in the morning when they arrived, so the lobby and restaurant were empty, and the night clerk did not seem to recognize Wallis from her photographs in the newspapers. Perhaps due to their sheer exhaustion or frayed nerves, they did not think to change the alias that had failed them at customs. Once again, they registered as "Mr. and Mrs. Harris."

Lord Brownlow escorted Wallis to her room. She thanked him profusely for being unwittingly involved in her terrible flight. Heartbroken and confused, she could no longer contain her emotions, and she collapsed on her bed and began to cry. She was consumed by memories. The winding, twisting, and confusing road of her life had been full of strange events and struggles, but nothing had prepared her for this. A king, and not just any king, but the most powerful monarch in the world, was about to walk away from his entire empire. Just for her. It was too much to even begin to contemplate. She was a long way from Baltimore, the Navy, and the uncomplicated life she had lived with Ernest before she met the Prince of Wales.

Her crying eventually turned to shaking sobs. Inconsolable and fearful of being alone, she called Lord Brownlow and asked him to stay with her as she cried herself to sleep.

AT ONE O'CLOCK IN THE MORNING, JUST AS WALLIS'S ferry was nearing the coast of France, the king left Buckingham Palace for the Fort. Walter Monckton insisted on accompanying him, fearing the king was slipping into a depression.

The crowd outside the palace had grown in numbers. As the king's car passed through the enormous wrought iron gates, he and Monckton could hear the unmistakable sound of cheering for him.

It was the last time he would leave the palace as King Edward VIII.

THE NEXT DAY, THE KING WAS INFORMED THE international press had arrived during the night and surrounded the Fort. Journalists were camped outside his entrance gates and hiding in the trees with cameras. The morning newspapers were filled with coverage of the crisis, but to the king's delight, it seemed public opinion was on his side.

The king immediately sent for George Allen as well as his most reliable telephone operator, William Bateman, and his royal courier, Major Ulick Alexander. Bateman moved into the telephone room to ensure the king's conversations were not intercepted and reported to the press. Alexander was tasked with transporting the box containing court papers back and forth between the Fort and Buckingham Palace.

The king waited anxiously for any word from London. The Cabinet was set to meet that morning at ten-thirty to discuss his radio broadcast. He was also nervously waiting to hear from Wallis. The first update he heard came from the editor of Reuters, who had learned of the debacle with the Buick's registration. He told the king that Wallis's whereabouts had been discovered and the press was chasing her to Cannes.

Shortly thereafter, William Bateman announced that Wallis was on the line with a bad connection from a place called Evreux. The king demanded to know why she was there. Evreux was way off the designated course. No one could answer the question, least of all Wallis, whom he could barely hear over the static on the line.

"What are you doing in Evreux? What are you doing in Evreux?" he yelled again and again until the connection was lost.

EARLIER THAT DAY, AT THE HOTEL DE LA POSTE, Wallis, still fully dressed from crying herself to sleep the night before, awoke to the sound of Lord Brownlow banging on her door. Their entire party had overslept. They had planned to leave at dawn, but now it was already mid-morning. Worse was the fact that they had been discovered by the press due to their error of registering as Mr. and Mrs. Harris again.

Wallis changed her clothes quickly, but there was no

chance of escaping the hotel unnoticed. Inspector Evans led her to the front door hoping there would not be a commotion, but her car was surrounded by journalists and curiosity seekers. As soon as they stepped outside, a French woman cried, "Voila la dame!" and picked up her camera. Inspector Evans knocked it out of her hands as Lord Brownlow shoved Wallis into the back seat.

"Whatever did you do that for?" Wallis cried.

"How could I be sure the girl did not have a pistol with her camera?" Inspector Evans replied.

The crowd erupted in an uproar as Ladbrook peeled away from the curb. Wallis told the men the only thing she wanted to do was telephone the king, and they had better find a place for her to do it. They took a detour to try to lose the reporters trailing behind them. The first stop they came to was the Hotellerie du Grand-Cerf in Evreux, Normandy. Wallis got out of the car with Lord Brownlow and she was relieved no one paid them any mind. They ducked into a telephone booth near the hotel's bar, and Wallis began jotting down notes about what she planned to say on a sheet of hotel stationery.

Lord Brownlow placed the call to the Fort and handed the receiver to Wallis. But the connection was so poor she could barely hear the king even though he was shouting about why they were in Evreux. She didn't want to take the time to explain because she wanted to get to the point. "On no account is Mr. James to step down," she said, using the code name they had designated for the king. "You must get advice," she said. You must bring in your old friends. See Duff Cooper. Talk to Lord Derby. Talk to the Aga Khan. Do nothing rash."

The king either ignored her or couldn't hear her. "What are you doing in Evreux?" he asked again.

"On no account is Mr. James to step down!"

"What are you doing in Evreux!"

It was hopeless. The more agitated she became, the more Lord Brownlow feared someone at the bar would hear her and realize who she was. Wallis finally gave up and put the receiver back on the hook.

❧

FIVE MILES DOWN THE ROAD, WALLIS began to think about the notes she had been using in the telephone booth. Primarily, she was reflecting on the fact that the notes were no longer in her pocket. She reached her hand in farther. Nothing. She checked the other pocket. Nothing. All their code names had been written on it. "Tornado" for Beaverbrook. "Crutch" for the prime minister, "WSC" for Winston Churchill, and "Mr. James" for the king. She had even scrawled, "Under no circumstances is Mr. James to step down."

Wallis began to panic. She overturned her purse onto the floor of the Buick.

Lord Brownlow stared at her, perplexed. "Lost something?" he asked.

"The notes." She dug through the contents of her purse. "The notes for my talk with the king. I must have left them in the booth."

Lord Brownlow exploded. "It would be unkind of me to say how like a woman, but Wallis, I will say it anyway. Now we are in a hole. If we go back, you're almost certain to be recognized this time."

They debated for a few moments. They could go back for the paper with the cryptic writing and risk being recognized or forget the notes because they were cryptic anyway, and who would ever put together a Mr. James stuck in a tornado with a crutch?

In the midst of the commotion, Ladbrook made a wrong turn.

⚜

No one in the car could figure out why the road signs were pointing them in the direction of Deauville. Deauville was on the north coast, an hour west of Dieppe where the ferry had docked.

Lord Brownlow leaned forward and asked Ladbrook if he was lost. Ladbrook denied it until they indeed pulled straight into Deauville. They had made nearly a full circle. Sheepishly, Ladbrook turned the car around and headed south.

They finally reached the central French town of Orleans at sunset and tried valiantly to find another telephone booth. They eventually located one at a hotel where a confused concierge tried to act discreet as the American woman in front of him kept trying to place a call to England. She tried for an hour to no avail.

BACK AT THE FORT, THE KING'S NERVES WERE QUICKLY becoming frayed. Wallis was lost in France, he was trapped in his castle because of the press outside, and Walter Monckton had just informed him the Cabinet rejected his request for the radio broadcast. Baldwin was due to arrive at the Fort that evening and there was nothing the king could do but sit and wait.

SNOW WAS FALLING IN FRANCE AND EVEN THOUGH the tension in the car had subsided after the wrong turn toward Deauville, everyone was exhausted. Wallis was depressed by her failure to reach the king, Ladbrook was tired after navigating country roads, and the weather was taking a turn for the worse. Lord Brownlow suggested they stop for dinner in a town called Blois.

When they pulled into the driveway of the Hotel de

France et de Guise the snowfall increased rapidly, and they decided they had better spend the night. No one realized the press had discreetly followed the car to Blois. Lord Brownlow went inside to check them in, and he was startled to find the French paparazzi camped in the lobby waiting for Wallis.

❧

As the evening progressed, the Fort was becoming more and more besieged. The telephone was ringing incessantly and couriers from London were coming and going almost constantly.

Baldwin arrived and met with the king in his office. He wanted the crisis to come to an end, and he urged the king to make a final decision—Wallis or your throne.

The king replied he would let him know when he, and he alone, was ready.

Unbeknownst to both men, a vehicle was racing toward the Fort with Winston Churchill at the wheel. As far as Churchill was concerned, all the debating about what the king should do was essentially a waste of time because Wallis could not remarry until after April 27 anyway as was mandated by the divorce court. If the king would just sit tight and wait it out, he could try again at a later date to convince the government to allow him to marry her morganatically.

The king received Churchill in the dining room at eight o'clock and agreed that Churchill did have a point. But waiting until April to broach the subject with the government again meant he would be coronated on May 12 without Wallis as his wife.

Churchill suggested the king pretend he was sick. He told the king to go to Windsor Castle and post doctors at the door so he could think everything over. Churchill's last words as he was leaving after midnight were: "Sir, it is time for reflection. You must allow time for the battalions to march." The king would later recall that Churchill made the monarchy alive for him once again and "suffused with light" when for days it had been a "dry and lifeless thing."

Later that night, the king paced aimlessly in his bedroom. Everything was a mess. In London, many people were protesting the government in favor of him. The newspapers were reporting that a "King's Party" was forming, yet the government was now threatening to resign if he did not give Wallis up. Alone, without advisors surrounding him, he somehow managed to convince himself that he was causing a civil war and was tearing apart his own kingdom.

In his memoirs he wrote: "The British Crown is the living symbol of Imperial unity and voluntary allegiance. It inspires unity. But it would no longer inspire unity if the man who wore it reigned over a community distressed and divided. True, I would still be King. But I would no longer be King by the free and common consent of all. The Crown would have lost, in consequence, much of its aura and beneficent usefulness. The cherished conception of the monarchy above politics would have been shattered, and the British party system might have suffered a fatal hurt. Could Wallis and I have hoped to find happiness under that condition? This was the question I answered in my soul that night. The answer was no."

When the king finally went to sleep, his mind was made up. He would walk away from the destiny he was born to live and the empire he was born to serve. He would take second place in the hierarchy of the monarchy and marry the woman he decided he could not live without. He would abdicate the throne and face the consequences of his action with courage and dignity.

Inconceivable to him at the time, the consequences were far beyond anything he anticipated. His life, as he knew it, was over.

THE NEXT MORNING, THE KING SUMMONED WALTER Monckton to his bedroom after breakfast. "I want you to go to London immediately and warn the prime minister that when he comes to the Fort this afternoon,

I shall notify him formally that I have decided to abdicate," the king told him.

Monckton tried to remain calm even though he was devastated by the news. He reminded the king that abdication meant the king would become a private citizen. He might no longer be able to rely on the monarchy the way he had for his entire life. The king assured him he understood. He planned to speak about his new status and his finances with his younger brother, Prince Albert, who would inherit the throne.

Monckton, realizing the king's mind was made up, suggested the king request a bill to allow him to marry Wallis immediately rather than having to wait another five months. The king agreed and Monckton left for London to plead the case.

The king summoned George Allen and asked him to travel to Switzerland to discreetly find him a hotel near Zurich. Baldwin had already requested that the king leave England if he abdicated to allow Prince Albert the chance to settle in as the country's new monarch. Baldwin suggested an exile of two years, after which he would be able to return to England to live at the Fort.

AT THREE O'CLOCK IN THE MORNING, A PORTER delivered coffee to Wallis's room at the hotel. She wanted to leave Blois early to make up for lost time.

With the press still stationed in the lobby, Wallis and her escorts had to sneak down the back staircase and through the kitchen to reach their car.

It was still snowing when they arrived in the town of Moulins. Lord Brownlow, aware that none of Wallis's phone calls had reached the king, sent a secret telegram to Walter Monckton attempting once again to encourage the king to just postpone the marriage, save his throne, and marry her once everyone calmed down.

Shortly after leaving Moulins, Wallis noticed the Buick was beginning to smell of whiskey. She turned and caught Lord Brownlow sniffing his coat. Wallis asked him to explain himself.

"I have suffered a major disaster," Lord Brownlow said. He had hidden a flask of whiskey in his coat pocket, which he had somehow managed to smash against the car door.

Wallis ordered him to open his window. While the whiskey drama was happening, Ladbrook lost his way again. When he finally pulled over to ask directions from a pedestrian outside of Lyon, another man shouted, "Voila la dame!" Once again, they were surrounded.

IN LONDON, MONCKTON ARRIVED AT THE government's headquarters at Number 10 Downing

Street to learn the result of the king's request for Wallis's immediate divorce. After waiting for two hours, the ministers finally called him into the room to inform him the proposal had been denied. When Monckton left, the last of the king's supporters screamed and cheered when they recognized the king's car.

Meanwhile, Churchill decided he would make a last plea to the save the king. He stood before the House of Commons and tried to reason with everyone, but he was quickly shouted off the stage.

৩১৩

IN FRANCE, THE PRESS WAS IN HOT PURSUIT OF Wallis's car as the party passed through Lyon and headed to the village of Vienne where Wallis was friendly with the owners of the Restaurant de la Pyramide. She knew they would give her sanctuary.

Once there, she finally reached the king by telephone in a private room. Not wanting to alarm her, the king said nothing to Wallis of his plans to abdicate even though his decision had been made.

When it came time to leave, Wallis and her escorts realized the press had encircled the main door. The owner suggested Wallis exit through a small window above a tiny sink in the basement kitchen. There was a driveway beneath the window, and they could jump down to the street.

Ladbrook maneuvered the car into the narrow drive-way, and Inspector Evans climbed through the window first and caught Wallis as she came down behind him. Then Lord Brownlow forced his way through. "Too bad Stanley Baldwin missed that little scene," he snapped. They were now only a day's journey from Cannes.

At eleven o'clock that evening, they pulled into the town of Brignoles. It was closed up for the night, but they decided they had better telephone Herman and Katherine Rogers. They were afraid the Rogers would assume Wallis had been delayed another day and lock the gates to their villa.

Lord Brownlow banged on the door of the post office in the hopes someone would be inside to let them use the telephone. Instead, a local man began yelling out his window. He called Lord Brownlow an idiot for not noticing the payphone in plain view across the street, and then hollered that he was even more of an idiot for telephoning someone in the middle of the night.

By the time he got to the payphone, Lord Brownlow was raging mad. He could barely speak French and the night operator did not understand him. He started cursing and pounding his fists against the phone box. Finally, he got a call through to the Rogers. They warned him there were reporters everywhere outside their villa.

A few hours later, Wallis hid under a car mat on the

backseat floor until they pulled safely through the gates of Villa Lou Viei. Herman and Katherine waited at the front door to welcome them.

THE ROGERS' VILLA, ONCE AN ANCIENT MONASTERY, was located on a hill above Cannes. It looked private, but when Wallis awoke the next morning, Katherine warned her to stay away from all the windows. The press had not only surrounded the gates of the villa, but they were camped out in the trees and on the hill with long-range camera lenses.

That day, the king kept calling the villa, but the lines were so full of static that any chance of having a meaningful conversation was futile. Still, the king and Wallis tried to speak to one another using the codes they had devised, knowing full well the conversation was being intercepted by eavesdroppers. When the king told her he planned to abdicate, Wallis panicked. She had left England so he would come to his senses and realize what he was giving up. She had hoped her departure would halt the events that were spiraling out of control, but now she realized she had been wrong. Despite their engagement, she still had trouble believing he had the nerve to go through with an abdication. She pleaded with him to just stop everything, but he told her his mind was made up.

Wallis then dashed off a rambling letter to him and sent it by airmail. She begged him to stay on the throne or at least wait before doing anything rash. She wanted him to recant everything he said to Baldwin about abdication. "I will repeat again what to say to Mr. Baldwin," she wrote. "I stand back of everything I have said but I do not wish create a situation within the country so I therefore will not press the issue at the moment but reopen it in the autumn." She figured that if he delayed the case until the fall, he would be able to revisit it with a clearer mind and better counsel. "Mr. Baldwin has misrepresented your case already in Parliament – by keeping repeating into their heads I must be Queen," she continued.

Her rationale was that if he presented the case at a later date after he had seemingly sacrificed Wallis for his crown, then the government and the public might be more receptive to a morganatic marriage. If not, he could abdicate then. At least by then her divorce mandate would be over, and he would have had time to work out his affairs. If he gave up the kingship, then he needed to thoroughly determine his pension and his title.

After she sent someone to mail her letter, she discussed everything with Lord Brownlow. He suggested she make a public statement that would prove what she had told him the night they left the Fort. She would break off her relationship with the king if it would save his throne.

Wallis called the king back. She explained she wanted the public to know she did not want the king to abdicate. The king wasn't pleased by the idea, but he seemed to understand her point. He didn't want Wallis to suffer indefinitely as the woman who destroyed the monarchy.

At seven o'clock, her statement was read to the press waiting outside Lou Viei.

Mrs. Simpson, throughout the last few weeks, has invariably wished to avoid any action or proposal which would hurt or damage His Majesty or the Throne. Today her attitude is unchanged, and she is willing, if such action would solve the problem, to withdraw forthwith from a situation that has been rendered both unhappy and untenable.

The press was satisfied. Some even speculated the statement had ended the abdication crisis. If the king was in a bind because he had engaged a woman and encouraged her to divorce her husband, and if he was too much of a gentleman to retract his proposal of marriage, then Wallis was the one who had to break off the relationship. And, apparently, she was willing to do just that.

Wallis went to sleep that night hopeful the crisis would be resolved.

WHEN BALDWIN HEARD THE STATEMENT, HE WAS perplexed by Wallis's action. If she ended her relationship with the king, then he would presumably want to stay on his throne. Otherwise, he would be abdicating for no reason. Baldwin was growing weary of the situation and he wanted everything resolved immediately once and for all. He contacted Wallis's divorce attorney, Theodore Goddard, and offered him use of his airplane so Goddard could fly to France to meet with Wallis.

Goddard was also confused by Wallis's statement and wondered if she wanted him to retract her divorce. He readily agreed to take the plane and he headed to the Fort to inform the king he was going to Cannes. Goddard reminded the king if Wallis withdrew her divorce then she was technically still married to Ernest. Therefore, the king should not put his throne in jeopardy for a woman who could not be his wife anyway.

The king was irritated. He believed Wallis's statement was fiction and crafted so she would not be blamed by the world. Besides, the king told him, it was too late. He was going to abdicate and marry Wallis, and he wanted the nonsense of Wallis withdrawing her divorce petition to stop. The king helped Goddard into his coat and told him not to go to France.

As far as the king was concerned, his reign would soon be over. Therefore, he had pressing issues he needed to resolve. He was concerned about his inheritance and title so he had asked Prince Albert to come to the Fort to go over the pragmatic subjects the abdication would soon present.

Goddard, meanwhile, disregarded the king's request and left for France anyway. He had never flown on an airplane before and he was nervous about his weak heart. He asked a doctor friend of his to accompany him, much to his relief as it turned out. Not only was the night stormy, but the plane kept encountering engine trouble and the pilot had to make several emergency landings.

When the king learned of Goddard's flight, he angrily phoned Wallis and told her that her attorney had gone mad. "I don't know what his purpose is. All I know is that Baldwin is behind it. Don't be influenced by anything Goddard says. Better still, do not see him at all." Wallis was baffled as to why her attorney was flying to France when he could have just used the telephone.

Then, just as she was about to go to bed, the press outside the villa presented a statement to Inspector Evans. *Mr. Goddard, the well-known lawyer who acts for Mrs. Simpson, has arrived at Marseilles by special plane. He brought with him Dr. Kirkwood, the well-known gynecologist, and his anesthetist.* The press was demanding an explanation. What was her lawyer doing with a gynecologist and anesthetist?

Wallis was as perplexed as the press and Lord Brownlow was furious. "Herman and I have done everything in our power to protect your dignity, your good name and peace of mind, and the prestige of the king," he said. "This is the last straw. Wallis, I'll deal with this." He stormed out of the villa, trying to think of something to say that would explain the situation.

❧

WHEN GODDARD FINALLY ARRIVED AT LOU VIEI THE next morning, he met with Wallis in the drawing room. Embarrassed by the pandemonium he caused, he apologized profusely and explained the doctor in question was an acquaintance he brought along because he was afraid to fly and feared he would have a heart attack. He asked Wallis if she was considering withdrawing her petition for divorce.

❧

THE KING WAS STILL TRYING TO WORK OUT HIS inheritance issue with Prince Albert when his brother Prince George appeared at the Fort.

"What the dickens are you doing here!" the king exclaimed. He was trying to keep the rest of his family out of his personal catastrophe.

"Whether you want to see me or not I have come," Prince George replied. He subsequently moved into the Fort. Shortly thereafter, Baldwin, Monckton, and a driver pulled up to the Fort in an impossibly small car.

They piled out of it, Baldwin lugging a suitcase behind him.

The king called one of his assistants into the room. "Did you see that thing in the hall?" he asked.

"You mean Mr. Baldwin's suitcase?"

"Correct. Why did he bring it?"

"I believe he expects to spend the night here."

The king was running out of patience, and the last thing he wanted was the prime minister as a houseguest. He asked that someone, anyone, politely inform Baldwin to leave in his "preposterous little beetle of a motorcar."

The king and Baldwin never met again.

❦

THE NEXT DAY, WALLIS TELEPHONED THE KING AND told him that after speaking at length with Goddard, she had indeed decided to withdraw her petition for a divorce.

"It is too late," the king told her. "The abdication documents are being drawn up. The Cabinet is meeting this very moment to act upon them. Of course, you can do whatever you wish. You can go wherever you want, to China, Labrador, or the South Seas. But wherever you go, I will follow you."

As soon as his call with Wallis ended, he handed Monckton his formal declaration of his intent to abdicate. Unwavering and content with his decision, he ordered Monckton to deliver it to Baldwin in London.

Shortly thereafter, a servant announced Queen Mary was on her way to the Fort. The king was about to have a fit. First all the business about calling off the divorce, and now his mother. She was one of the last people he wanted at the Fort. He ordered an assistant to stop her car and have her meet him instead at Prince Albert's residence in Windsor Great Park.

When the king arrived there, as he expected, Queen Mary made one last attempt to reason with him. He told her as gently as possible his decision was final.

He arrived back at the Fort to find George Allen in a state of panic. Wallis's friend, Esmond Hammond, who had first proposed the morganatic marriage weeks before, had also appeared at Lou Viei to try to convince Wallis to withdraw her divorce petition.

"Do you mean that I have to go through all that again?" the king exclaimed.

AT THE VILLA, A NERVOUS AND AGITATED WALLIS WAS paralyzed by anxiety. After her visit from Goddard, Hammond arrived unexpectedly. She was more befuddled than ever. The king was insisting on abdicating, her lawyer and Hammond were telling her to withdraw her divorce petition, and her friends were insisting she should ignore Goddard and Hammond because the king was going to abdicate anyway. Now all she wanted was to leave Europe altogether. She ordered Lord Brownlow to book her on a ship from Genoa and to arrange a private train car to take her to the ship.

She then began to draft a new statement for the press explaining she was removing herself entirely from the Continent. But before she was able to issue it, the king reached her by telephone. "I can't seem to make you understand the position," he said. "It's all over. The Instrument of Abdication is already prepared."

When the call was over, everyone waited for Wallis to say something, but she was stunned into silence. And the question that still lingered in her mind was "Why me?" Why had he chosen her when he could have had anyone? "My endowments were definitely on the scanty side," she wrote. "Nobody ever called me beautiful or even pretty. I was thin in an era when a certain plumpness was a girl's ideal. My jaw was clearly too big and too pointed to be classic. My hair was straight where the laws of compensation might at least have provided curls...No one has ever accused me of being intellectual."

It was a question that would haunt her forever.

THE NEXT DAY, DECEMBER 10, 1936, THE KING SIGNED the Instrument of Abdication in the octagonal drawing room at the Fort. He then left for Windsor Castle where he would say goodbye to his former subjects over the radio. Since he was no longer a reigning monarch, the government could not prevent him from making a radio address.

At Lou Viei, everyone sat around the radio in the sitting room to hear the former king's voice crackle across the airwaves from Great Britain.

"AT LONG LAST I AM ABLE TO SAY A FEW WORDS OF my own.

I have never wanted to withhold anything, but until now it has not been constitutionally possible for me to speak.

A few hours ago, I discharged my last duty as King and Emperor, and now that I have been succeeded by my brother, the Duke of York, my first words must be to declare my allegiance to him. This I do with all my heart.

You all know the reasons which have impelled me to renounce the Throne, but I want you to understand that in making up my mind I did not forget the country or the empire, which, as Prince of Wales and lately as King, I have for 25 years tried to serve.

But you must believe me when I tell you that I have found it impossible to carry the heavy burden of responsibility and to discharge my duties as King, as I would wish to do, without the support and help of the woman I love, and I want you to know that the decision I have made has been mine, and mine alone. This was a thing I had to judge for myself. The other person most nearly concerned has tried, up to the last, to persuade me to take a different course. I have made this, the most serious decision of my life, only upon a single thought of what would in the end be best for all.

This decision has been made less difficult to me by the sure knowledge that my brother, with his long training in the public affairs of this Country and with his fine qualities, will be able to take my place forthwith without interruption or injury to the life and progress of the Empire, and he has one matchless blessing, enjoyed by so many of you, and not bestowed on me, a happy home with his wife and children.

During those hard days, I have been comforted by my mother and by my family.

The Ministers of the Crown, and in particular Mr. Baldwin, the prime minister, have always treated me with full consideration. There has never been any constitutional difference between me and them and between me and Parliament. Bred in the constitutional traditions by my father, I should never have allowed any such issue to arise.

Ever since I was Prince of Wales, and later on when I occupied the throne, I have been treated with the greatest kindness by all classes of people, wherever I have lived or journeyed throughout the Empire. For that, I am very grateful.

I now quit altogether public affairs, and I lay down my burden. It may be some time before I return to my native land, but I shall always follow the fortunes of the British race and Empire with profound interest, and if, at any time in the future, I can be found of service to His Majesty in a private station, I shall not fail.

And now we all have a new King.

I wish him and you, his people, happiness and prosperity with all my heart.

God bless you all.

God Save The King."

WHEN HE FINISHED SPEAKING, WALLIS REMAINED frozen in place on the sofa. She covered her face so no one in the room could see her tears.

EPILOGUE

After the abdication, the former king retreated that same evening to Austria where he stayed with friends in a castle near Vienna. Wallis remained in France at Lou Viei before moving to Chateau de Cande near Tours where they were eventually married. No member of the royal family attended the ceremony. In the early years after the abdication, the Duke of Windsor made repeated requests to return home to the Fort and serve his country in some capacity, but he was always refused. Queen Mary perhaps best summarized the sentiment of the royal family regarding the abdication in a letter she wrote him in July of 1938. *I do not think you have ever realized the shock which the attitude you took up caused your family and the whole Nation. It seemed inconceivable to those who had made such sacrifices during the war that you, as their King, refused a lesser sacri-*

fice...The feeling about your marriage is far deeper and wider than you seem to realize, and your return to England would only mean division and controversy. The Fort was shuttered and abandoned, its grounds overgrown, and its former glory diminished to an empty shell of a castle. When World War II broke out, the British government did award the Duke an official position, but it was one quite as far away from the action as they could manage— Governor of the Bahamas. After the war, he finally accepted he would never again return to the glories of his former life. As private citizens, the Duke and Duchess of Windsor became society figures known for their lavish entertaining, extensive travel, and exquisite manner of dress and style. They eventually retired to France and remained there until their deaths, he in 1972, and she in 1986.

A FEW FINAL WORDS

Ten years ago, this small book was privately published as a limited edition for the members of the Duke and Duchess of Windsor Historical Society. It is an introduction only, a primer to a woman who was always intent on moving forward and making the best of her circumstances. At the time, the story of the Windsors seemed rather forgotten. Most of the books I used for my research were found collecting dust on a shelf at the Strand bookstore in New York City.

Frankly, I'd always found the story of the abdication rather absurd. When the king walked away from the throne in 1936, the world was in the midst of a Great Depression. Two years before, Hitler breached the 1919 Treaty of Versailles that ended World War I when he expanded the size of his army. In March of 1936, a newly rearmed Hitler ordered the invasion of the Rhineland.

Clearly, the embers that sparked World War II were starting to flicker on the horizon. It is difficult not to think, by golly, weren't there bigger problems out there than who the king wanted to marry? And, really, what difference did it make who was queen?

Yet, something about Wallis's story intrigued me—an impoverished, Navy wife with aristocratic roots who ended up divorced and alone until her second husband saved her and she moved to London where she befriended the Prince of Wales who gave up his throne for her. As I researched her journey, it was obvious she faced trials and tribulations, yet she never lost her inner spirit and love of life. The action of the world was happening in one place—where she was at the time.

One Sunday afternoon, I took a drive to Warrenton, Virginia where she waited out her divorce from Win at the Warren Green Hotel. The town was small and quaint, and the hotel she lived in is now a civic building. I walked through the lobby and found a small photograph of her hanging on a wall near the staircase. All I could think was: *Here?* The closest confidant, companion, and wife of King Edward VIII lived *here?*" I wondered if she ever imagined when she was alone in the dingy hotel room that she would rise again, so high as to marry the King of England.

I am often asked what I think "Wallis Simpson" was really like, especially in light of recent biographies that speculate about potentially sensational aspects of her life. I always reply that I view her as a master of rein-vention and a model of self-discipline rather than a scandalous, intruding woman who never should have moved in the Prince of Wales's circle in the first place. Through that lens, following are my answers to many of the other questions I receive about her:

When did they first meet?

There is controversy over this because their memoirs contain incorrect dates. However, Wallis's letter to her Aunt Bessie dated January 8, 1931, and continued on January 13, 1931, indicates the date of their first meeting was January 10, 1931, at Thelma's house in Melton Mowbray. Wallis was excited to have met the Prince of Wales, and she had no reason to falsify a date in a letter to her aunt.

Was she a ruthless social climber?

A social climber, yes. Ruthless, no. She was an expa-triate in London, and she was desperately lonely in her new city. She loved entertaining and she was thrilled that her flat became a salon for her fascinating and cosmopolitan new friends.

Did she seduce the Prince of Wales?

Over a period of five years, she became his best friend and closest, honest, tell-it-like-it-is confidant. He was surrounded by sycophants, fawners, and flatterers.

Wallis was an extrovert, outspoken and friendly, and not intimidated by his position even though she respected it. She was a breath of fresh air for him. They were friends first, lovers later.

Was she scheming to be queen?

No. Wallis wanted an exciting life and, even though the Prince of Wales was a stark contrast to his staid, Victorian-era parents, the monarchy was stifling and hopelessly outdated. For Wallis, being as she was an independent American woman, becoming queen was akin to a prison sentence. She enjoyed the more thrilling role of being the king's mistress and best friend.

Also, there is rather damning evidence in a letter from Wallis to the king that points to the fact that neither one of them wanted anything to do with the throne, though of course they never admitted it. In the letter she wrote on December 6, 1936, the one she airmailed to him before the abdication, she mentions two plans they had discussed, both of which almost definitely lead him to abdication. His plan was to abdicate right away. Her plan entailed that he serve his country as king for eight months and then try again for a morganatic marriage. If he was refused then, "we have the glorious other [plan]," she wrote. That "glorious plan" was abdication.

But it is important to remember that neither of

them expected he would be exiled for life if he abdicated. The king believed he would be able to return home in a couple of years and live the royal life of a duke in service to his country. They may have developed a new plan altogether if they knew abdication meant a lifetime of banishment.

Did she love him?

After their romance began, they were nearly inseparable. Their letters to each other are filled with romanticism and tender expressions. She made it her life's mission to ensure that his every need was catered to in the manner of which he was accustomed. She recreated a miniature kingdom for him even though he was no longer king. That was certainly a grand gesture of love.

Furthermore, she did not marry him at gunpoint. After he abdicated, they had to wait six months before they could wed according to her divorce decree. She easily could have booked passage on an ocean liner to anywhere in the world as she later claimed she had always planned to do. There was nothing stopping her. The ex-king had already provided for her financially for the rest of her life so it was not a question of money. And even if she felt obligated to marry him after the abdication debacle, she easily could have filed for divorce at a later date and moved on with her life. I think it is safe to say she loved him.

Did she possess exotic powers over men that she learned in China?

This question started because, as her relationship with the Prince of Wales became serious, British government officials began to pay attention to her. Someone started a rumor about a file called the "China Dossier" that proved she was a sorceress who hypnotized the prince with her boudoir techniques. This dossier has never surfaced, and even if it does, it is surely exaggerated fiction written by people who feared she would be their next queen.

Was she a man or hermaphrodite?

No. I wish I didn't have to address such nonsense here, but it comes up often in lurid accounts of her. This is another rumor that was started to defame her, likely for personal gain of book sales and press coverage. Because of her unconventional beauty, she was an easy target for that particular fabrication.

Did she have other affairs besides the Prince of Wales after their romance began?

It's possible. The world changed after World War I, and people lived for the moment. She was in her thirties when she met the prince with one failed marriage already behind her. Ernest Simpson may have saved her from the relative poverty of her childhood and her struggles after her separation from Win Spencer, but

Ernest, however solid, loyal, and secure, might have been too stable for the fun-loving Wallis. After her move to London, she may have enjoyed the company of other men. Ernest, with his insistence on weekly household budgeting and his financial stress due to the Great Depression, probably did bore Wallis a little. But the affairs, if there were any, were most likely commonplace and unimportant to her story and life journey.

Why wasn't she titled Her Royal Highness, but he was titled His Royal Highness?

The royal family punished him for abdicating by denying his wife the royal prefix. But, by not granting her those three little letters, they ended up torturing everyone, including themselves, because it caused confusion anytime the Windsors attended an event abroad that required protocol. The duke was steamed about it for the rest of his life, but the duchess probably cared less about a meaningless title. If it bothered her, it was only because it bothered him so much. In the royal family's defense for what now seems like silly pettiness, given what was going on in the world, the king picked a heck of a time to start planning a wedding.

Was the duke a Nazi sympathizer?

This question is a little more ambiguous because one has to take into consideration the mindset of the 1930s. Like Charles Lindbergh, Joseph Kennedy, and many others, the Duke was a victim of history and the duplicity of Hitler in the years leading up to the war. The Nazi propaganda machine did a clever job of using famous international people to validate their economic and military advances while totally avoiding political and human rights issues.

Today, it seems largely forgotten that the House of Windsor was actually the Germanic House of Saxe-Coburg and Gutha until the Duke's father changed their family name after WWI in response to anti-German sentiment. The British royal family had German ancestry and German relatives. World War I notwithstanding, Germany was a special place to the Duke and the royal family.

Was the duke pro-German? Yes. Was he pro-peace? Yes. Was he political? No. In the 1930's no one except Hitler and his military wanted another war. The duke and duchess did travel to Germany to meet with Hitler, but it was an ill-conceived peace tour. So, was the duke pro-Nazi and pro-Hitler then? This question is a bit more complex. The duke was fascinated by Hitler's immense organizational skills and his strategies for advancing industrial labor during the height of the worldwide Depression. And Hitler's economic revitalization of Germany after World War I was considered impressive. Even *Time* magazine named Hitler "Man of the Year" in 1938. Also, the Duke wrongly assumed that if there was an enemy out there, it was the Soviet

Union, based on the violent overthrow of the Russian monarchy during World War I. The duke viewed Germany as a potential ally against such a threat until 1939 when Hitler's intent to start another war became apparent with his invasion of Poland. Almost immediately thereafter, the duke showed his loyalty to Great Britain by entering wartime service, first as a major-general with the British Military Mission in France, then as Governor of the Bahamas.

What was so special about her that a king gave up his throne?

Perhaps somewhat sadly I always come back to one simple question—had she been an heiress to a grand fortune or a stunningly beautiful woman, would anyone have ever questioned his love for her?

NOTES

The primary sources used for *The King and Mrs. Simpson* were the respective memoirs of the Duke and Duchess of Windsor:

Windsor, Duchess of. *The Heart Has Its Reasons: The Memoirs of the Duchess of Windsor*: The Companion Book Club, 1958.

Windsor, Duke of. *A King's Story: The Memoirs of the Duke of Windsor*. New York: G.P. Putnam's Sons, 1947.

Departure

The descriptions of Fort Belvedere, the characters involved, their dialogue and the evening of December 3, 1936, are found in the Duke and Duchess of Windsor's memoirs. The conversation between the Duke of Windsor and Mrs. Merryman comes from the Duke of Windsor's memoirs.

The Prince

The meeting between the Duke and Duchess of Windsor comes from the Duchess of Windsor's memoirs. The works that were used in this section to describe the Duke of Windsor's childhood, his time at the Royal Navy College, Oxford, World War I, his world travels, and the 1920s include the Duke of Windsor's memoirs and the following: Bolitho, Hector. *King Edward VIII: An Intimate Biography*. New York: The Literary Guild Club of America, 1937; Donaldson, Frances. *Edward VIII*. New York: J.B. Lippincott, 1974; Fromkin, David. *Europe's Last Summer*. New York: Random House, 2005; Gilbert, Martin. *A History of the Twentieth Century: Volume 1*. New York: Avon Books, 1997; and Ziegler, Philip. *King Edward VIII*. New York: Knopf, 1991.

Wallis

All details regarding the Duchess of Windsor's childhood, marriage to Lt. Spencer, time spent in Washington, DC, Warrenton, VA, China, meeting and marriage to Ernest Simpson, and early years in London, come from the following sources: first and foremost, the Duchess of Windsor's memoirs; also consulted were: Bloch, Michael, ed. *Wallis and Edward: Letters 1931-1937*, New York: Summit Books, 1986; Higham, Charles. *The Secret Life of the Duchess of Windsor*. Hoboken: John Wiley & Sons, 2005; King, Greg. *The Duchess of Windsor:*

The Uncommon Life of Wallis Simpson. New York: Citadel, 1999; Martin, Ralph G. *The Woman He Loved.* New York: Simon & Schuster, 1973. The description of her meeting with the Prince of Wales is from the Duchess of Windsor's memoirs.

The King & Mrs. Simpson

The information regarding the presentation of debutantes at the royal court is from the Duke of Windsor's memoirs. The description of the blossoming friendship and relationship between the Duke and Duchess is from their respective memoirs. The details surrounding the death of King George V are from the Duke of Windsor's memoirs. Prime Minister Baldwin's reaction to King Edward VIII's ascension to the throne was described in Ziegler, Philip. *King Edward VIII.* New York: Knopf, 1991; and Williams, Susan. *The People's King.* London: Allen Lane, 2003. Also from the Duke & Duchess of Windsor's memoirs and the works by Williams and Ziegler are the descriptions regarding the escalation of the relationship between the Duke and Duchess of Windsor, the divorce proceedings between the Duchess of Windsor and Mr. Simpson, and the first few months of King Edward VIII's reign. Mr. Bloch's edited letters between the Duke and Duchess of Windsor were invaluable in this area. The details surrounding the origin of the Duke of Windsor's abdication process came from his memoirs and also the memoirs of Lord Beaverbrook. *The Abdication of Edward VIII*. London: Hamish Hamilton, 1966.

Flight to France

The events occurring between December 3, 1936 and December 10, 1936, when the Duke of Windsor officially renounced his throne, came from the Duke and Duchess of Windsor's memoirs in entirety.

Epilogue

The lines from Queen Mary's letter to the Duke of Windsor are from Ziegler, Philip. *King Edward VIII*. New York: Knopf, 1991. Wallis's letters are from Bloch, Michael, ed. *Wallis and Edward: Letters 1931-1937*, New York: Summit Books, 1986.

SUGGESTIONS FOR FURTHER READING

The Heart Has Its Reasons
   by The Duchess of Windsor.

Behind Closed Doors: The Tragic, Untold Story of the Duchess of Windsor
   by Hugo Vickers.

The Woman He Loved
   by Ralph Martin.

The Duchess of Windsor
   by Michael Bloch. *(for the photographs)*

Wallis & Edward: Letters 1931-1937
   edited by Michael Bloch.

ACKNOWLEDGMENTS

I wish to thank the following individuals for their extraordinary support of this book: my loving husband, Jean-Claude Lanza; Mark Gaulding and the members of the Duke and Duchess of Windsor Historical Society; all my wonderful friends and readers; Donald de Fano, my lifelong friend and former professor of English literature who kindly provided me with tremendous feedback on the art of creative nonfiction; Judy Roth, my talented and meticulous editor; my late grandmother, Mrs. Frances Terrill, who recounted the romance between King Edward VIII and Mrs. Simpson in great detail for me, and whose voice still echoes in my heart every day; my baby sister, "Milly", who never wants to hear about the Windsors again, but whose painstaking comments on my manuscript were invaluable; my father, a brilliant historian and the person who first gave me the vision to see the magic of the past; and my mother, whose artwork graces the cover, and without whom this book would not be a reality.

ABOUT THE AUTHOR

ERIN SCHULZ

Erin Frances Schulz is an American writer who was born in Newport, Rhode Island. She holds a baccalaureate in history from Fordham University in New York City and a postgraduate degree in international affairs from American University's School of International Service. She is also a graduate of the Swiss finishing school, Institut Villa Pierrefeu. She lives in Florida.

Printed in Great Britain
by Amazon

32295623R00088